T0132178

CREPUSCULAR DAWN

Copyright 2002 Semiotext(e)
All rights reserved.

This work, published as part of a program of aid for publication, received support
from the French Ministry of Foreign Affairs and the Cultural Service of the French
Embassy in the United States.

Excerpts from this book were first published in *Grey Room* #3,The MIT Press, Spring
2001 ("After Architecture: A Conversation"); *Made in USA* #3, 2001 ("Unmade in
USA") and *Pataphysics*, Psychomilitary issue, 2002 ("The Genetic Bomb").

Special Thanks to Giancarlo Ambrosino, Emily Lacy for copy editing; Mark Dery for
his erudition; Steve Argüelles for his musical expertise; Sanford Kwinter and Eran
Neuman for their judicious comments; and Hedi El Kholti for his helpful sugges-
tions. Finally, the authors would like to thank Chris Kraus for her suggestion of
the title.

This book is a project of the Semiotext(e) Institute for Outposthumanist Studies.

Semiotext(e)
2571 W. Fifth Street
Los Angeles, CA 90057
www.semiotexte.org

Semiotext(e)
501 Philosophy Hall
Columbia University
New York, NY 10027

Cover Photography: Stephanie Meckler © 2002
Design: Hedi El Kholti

ISBN: 978-1-58435-013-2
Distributed by The MIT Press, Cambridge, Mass. and London, England

CREPUSCULAR DAWN

PAUL VIRILIO / SYLVERE LOTRINGER

Translated by Mike Taormina

SEMIOTEXT(E) FOREIGN AGENTS SERIES

CONTENTS

INTRODUCTION

TIME BOMB

1.WARTIME

As the oxymoron in the title of this book indicates, there's something deeply ambivalent about Virilio's work and it is impossible to shrug it away in any simple way. Actually this ambivalence deserves to be looked at more closely: it is so thoroughly embedded in his writing (or, alternatively, in the nature of his enquiry) that most of his readers will be shocked again and again to realize that this prodigious prophet of speed, undoubtedly the most important thinker of technology since Martin Heidegger, actually hates technology with a passion. And yet passion there is, possibly stronger even than hate, and so infectious that this absolute rejection of technology could also be experienced as a form of love, or devotion. In any case, it is a very powerful bond, and he certainly couldn't have done what he did without it. Virilio's world is a crepuscular one, but so flamboyant and poetic that it could easily be mistaken for a new dawn.

Virilio often reminds us of the bombardments he was subjected to as a child in Normandy during WWII. Paradoxically these bombs weren't coming from the Germans who occupied France, but from the Allies who were trying to liberate it. So death was coming from both sides (a little girl he knew, a neighbor, was shot by a German patrol after curfew). It was war itself, and its impact on the populations, not just the German army, that became the enemy. This wanton destruction had a powerful impact on Virilio's sensibility. It remained the "primal scene" for his lifelong obsession with war. Like any traumatic event, war remains at the center of his preoccupations, and he has been looking for it everywhere with anticipation, with dread, with excitement. Only war can match war in intensity. However much you hate it, it becomes the means by which you connect creatively to the world.

Many people felt crushed by this overwhelming violence and its aftermath (the news coming from the extermination camps, the horrors disclosed), but war seems on the contrary to have had on Virilio a bracing effect, as if it had been some kind of rite of passage, his entry in adulthood. The war made him touch base with reality. Reviewing a book in 1947, Georges Bataille said something of the kind, praising its author, David Rousset, a French resistant deported to a forced labor camp, for having been "exalted, almost euphoric, at the thought of participating in a demented experiment." And Bataille dropped this terrible sentence: "Nothing more virile, nothing more *healthy*."[1] This comment still makes me shudder today and, of course, it was meant to have this effect on the reader. Yet I could never have written that myself. It wasn't the kind of war I had experienced as a child (I am six years younger than Virilio, and Jewish). The war added some value to Rousset's life, instead of taking away any possible sense of humanity. Virilio's reaction to the war seems to have been similarly "virile," and healthy. Like Rousset, touching the bottom made him realize that a truth was there begging to be unraveled. And he has been going for it ever since.

It is not surprising then that Virilio's first book, *Bunker Archeology*[2], would have documented the German blockhouses that dotted the Atlantic beaches after the war like so many cryptic dolmens or Paleolithic caves. (They proved as futile in the long run as the Maginot Line painstakingly built by the French to contain the German *Blitzkrieg*). Virilio must have spent a long time photographing this architecture of war along the coast all the way up to Belgium, although I suspect that he paid far more attention to the violence they contained in their thick wombs than to their baroque architecture. As will become clear in the first part of this book, it is not architecture itself that fascinates Virilio, but the *archeology of violence*, of which it is a part. I remember as a child climbing on these huge whales of concrete stranded on the beach and rolling down their smooth flanks to the sand below, like a human bomb. The last war was hardly over and we were already training for the war to come. Occasionally I would put my ear against the bunkers' hardened shell to catch the roar of war still trapped inside.

Bunker Archeology reads like an archeology of Virilio's mind. (It is fitting, of course, that he is claustrophobic and never travels anywhere). Like the bunkers themselves keeping close watch on the sky at the edge of the entire continent, he keeps surveying the horizon of our shrinking world, eager to pick up advanced signs of our impending doom. "I try to be," he said, "a kind of periscope of probable catastrophes." And the claustrophobic image of the bunker kept growing bigger and bigger over time until it literally absorbed the entire planet. This is also the curve this book intends to follow, from a bunker in space to a bunker in time. Like a time bomb, this *time bunker* is all the more ominous for being invisible. And so is the biological bomb born of the cyberworld, that is now threatening to take over where the atomic threat left off.

The terrors of war can't easily be forgotten. However hard you fight them in the dead of night, you know that the day will come when they will blast their way again into your life, *and you can't wait for it to happen*. There's nothing that stimulates the instinct of survival more and the "total mobilization" (as Ernst Junger would say) of one's senses, than these constructed cataclysms. No wonder Virilio, in his work, consistently adopted von Clausewitz's strategy of going to extremes. For the Prussian theorist, war always has a tendency to go beyond all limits and achieve total destruction unless politics steps in to prevent its complete release. But what happens when nothing is capable anymore of stopping the war machine that we have become ourselves on a global scale?

War isn't what it used to be. Obviously there is still plenty left of the good old ways all over the world, enough to fill our daily quota of massacres. For the most part, though, it has moved from steamy battlefields to a seamless process of preparation and organization. This *logistical* mutation, the "technological surprise" brought about by WWI, resulted in a war economy which keeps pursuing war by other means in times of war as well in times of peace. In a trans-political world like ours, it has become far more difficult, if not impossible, to check war's infernal tendency toward escape. We may well be reaching the point of no return—or rather it is this point itself that is now escaping us. If war in all its forms, from the more explicit to the more imperceptible, has now become intractable, there is nothing left for the theorist of pure war but to adopt the very same tendency. This is *the politics of the very worst*[3] that Virilio has stubbornly defended against all reasonable objections—"Why are you always so negative?"—in order to pursue his crepuscular enquiry. If war isn't in war anymore, for everyone to see, but buried in respectable laboratories and well-funded research agencies, science and knowledge themselves should cease to be considered above the fray. Technology is extending the reach of war exponentially—not just a war against entire populations, but a war of the human race against itself. This kind of delirium should be addressed for what it is, not with letter-bombs (Virilio is no Unabomber), or with terrorist threats, but from within knowledge itself. This is the line of thought that we started exploring together in *Pure War* twenty years ago[4] and it is given full scope here in relation to the "*biological bomb*" conceived both archeologically, through an investigation of its eugenic roots, and prospectively, by going to the limits of the unimaginable *which is already a reality*.

2.WAR ON TIME

Working as an architect in Paris in the mid-60s, Paul Virilio, together with Claude Parent, led the Architecture Principe group in elaborating their plans for a new psycho-physical form of architecture. In 1966, they published a series of manifestos urging architecture to begin again (*principium*) by establishing different architectonic rules at once geophysical and geometrical. Instead of insisting on balance and stability, architects would deliberately cultivate disequilibrium and fluctuation as a way of enhancing human mobility and consciousness.Humans, they claimed, were becoming too passive and sedentary in a world invaded by "dynamic vehicles" and it was up to architecture to set the body in motion again by using terrestrial gravitation like a motor. The group's program, which they called "Oblique

Function," was a calculated response to the crisis which they saw affecting all human activities, dwarfing body movements and threatening to bring about the mutation of mankind. Instead of merely housing "uprooted man," the new "oblique" dwellings of the post-industrial meta-city would contain obstacles such as curves, ramps, and planes inclined to varying degrees that would throw the user into action. "The natural dynamic of this situation," Virilio concluded, "will achieve what social theories failed to accomplish: the invention of a new society."

Whatever their ideological differences—and they seemed irreducible at the time—the various groups that were active in Paris in the mid-60s shared a common vision on the abrupt change brought about by the new "consumer society." All were striving in their own way to offset the destabilizing effects of technological advance and the massive impact of the new economy on daily life. Class struggles used to be located in the factories, now they would have to be fought at home. Early on, Henri Lefèbvre, a liberal Marxist sociologist, had warned against the invasion of everyday life by the "commodity." Now reaching its "final stage," capital was reinventing itself from scratch as a benevolent, even an exciting system. With the help of developing technologies, like domestic appliances, it was now trading its repressive antics for more "humane" and attractive forms of exploitation. Those it used to enslave as workers now were being reinvented as consumers. The nature and scope of "alienation," as a result, was changing drastically. What mattered most at this point was to instill in workers *desires* that the industry itself would satisfy. Flooded with material signs, the population at large was quickly shedding class distinctions and political ideologies and turning into a resilient, newly mobile mass of consumers.

For Virilio and Parent, the main function of the obliquity they advocated was to tear consumers away from their neutrality by inducing in them "a state of refusal and repulsion." Antonin Artaud had already devised a similar strategy in the mid-30s, a "theater of cruelty" meant to shock spectators out of their passivity though a bombardment of the senses. In its attempt to pre-empt the upcoming threat, Architecture Principe was updating the Modernist tradition which borrowed the rituals and instruments of religion to oppose it. But mental shocks and shrieks weren't sufficient anymore to reclaim the body and forge new collective bonds. For the Situationists, "integration" and "separation" were the major features of the "alienation" that was now affecting the entire society. *Integration*, because it homogenized social relations by means of images precluding any direct experience of life; *separation*, because everything that capital was making available through the technological breakthrough and justified in the name of progress—automobile, television, travel, etc.—merely reinforced the conditions of social isolation. The "spectacle" was both the primary *feature* of contemporary society and its main *instrument*, an active force of integration which precluded any real form of dialogue or participation.

The Situationists tried to loosen up the hold of the "society of spectacle" on people's lives by constructing ephemeral "situations" experienced collectively, a process of continual reinvention of their own consciousness in the face of the commodity. Architecture Principe, more down-to-earth, rather went for the body, and they went about it quite differently. One of the effects of the "spectacle" was to isolate people at home in front of their televisions, among the technological extensions of their own body. It was therefore in their own domestic setting that new devices had to be implanted in order restore their motricity, hopefully turning resistance to gravity into a new form of dance. As architects, Virilio and his group looked for more permanent ways of freeing the body from the multiple "prostheses," from cars to elevators, that were turning humans into a "motor handicap." Instead of sending them "drifting" through the city, as the Situationists did, they set them loose *in their own drifting environment*. But they couldn't do that without rethinking entirely the nature of the traditional habitat, whose verticality (walls, individual rooms, etc.) was reinforcing at home the separation and integration massively imposed outside. Instead, they devised an open topology based on the meta-stability of a "living ground" meant to collapse the opposition between inside and outside. They imagined new forms of "habitable circulation" promoting unstable and "unitary" situations that would insure the mobility in space of this last "metabolic vehicle," the body.

Reinforced houses and stabilized tanks, the bunkers reenacted the proto-history of ancient warfare by resisting the enemy's siege with weapons of obstruction. Architecture Principe similarly sought to recreate this type of defensive architecture, an architecture which resists its users by setting obstacles. In this sense, the "Oblique Function" was, in its own way, a tactical form of warfare. And yet, as the rebellion of May '68 amply demonstrated (Virilio actively participated in it), even barricading oneself in the streets or overturning cars, entering wide-eyed the poetics of ancient revolutions, was not enough anymore to check the seduction of consumerism, let alone turn back the clock. Like the body itself, the entire society was now being permeated by a flow of signs that substituted for things, as artificial respiration takes over patients' breathing in a coma. In the studio reality, politics was turned into a "motion picture." And yet even Guy Debord hadn't really grasped what was so powerful about the pictures he denounced. It wasn't their sheer accumulation that mattered most in the spectacle, but their *motion*. Hyperreality wasn't an ideological manipulation, as conspiracy theory would have it, *it was the product of speed*, of the dizzying instantaneity and interactivity of images.

The Situationists still believed that the invasion of the body politics by images had been engineered by the wealthy at the expense of the working class. What their analysis left out is that wealth is always an aspect of speed. All power is primarily "dromocratic" (from *dromos*, race), since it must rely on transport and transmission to control its territory. Dromocracy itself was power, not just the state, or wealth. The primary mechanism of social transformation was circulation, and even stasis had become a product of speed. "Polar inertia" was simply signs turned panic and pandemic—it was like being plugged to the wall, like a TV set. Moving from topology to tele-topology and from a defensive strategy to a more offensive—or at least *pre-emptive*—one, Virilio endeavored not only to offset the effects of technology obliquely, by manipulating space: he wanted to re-appropriate the knowledge released involuntarily by light-speed weapons of communication. Only by extrapolating the destructive bent inherent in instant technology could its riddle be unraveled. Yet Virilio's overwhelming preoccupation with interruptions and obstacles, with the revealing character of the accident still harks back to the strategies he proposed much earlier as an architect. Watching for the Total Accident, Virilio ambivalently remains at heart a High Modernist.

This Total Accident isn't just threatening humanity from the outside—an atomic meltdown of cosmic proportions, or a global electronic storm—it is intravenously released into the human race itself by the "genetic bomb," born out of speed (computers)

16

and biotechnology. It is no longer possible to reinforce the body-bunker's concrete walls against attack, the enemy already is inside. After a hundred thousand years of dormancy, the human race is about to jump boldly once again into an evolution of its own making whose consequences are still unfathomable. If the effects of "progress" on the biosphere over the last half-century can be any indication, the biological pollution now in the offing—from micro-engineering to body implants, endo and exo-farming species for organ replacement, bricolage of transgenic monsters, cloning of cells, etc.—should be greeted with a sense of awe, even if one doesn't believe that the human body had necessarily reached its final stage. The assault on the human race is too reminiscent of ethno-genocidal horrors for anyone to trust the neutrality of science or the global economic system. As Virilio's work shows, even a lonely periscope can make a difference at a time when differences themselves are being cultivated in a Petri dish.

Sylvère Lotringer

I

TIME BUNKER

1. ARCHEOLOGY

Space of War □ Bunkers □ Topology □ Oblique Function □ Dancing Staircase □ Slow Motion Catastrophe □ Resistance of the Body □ Walking City □ Entering Space-Time

In Architecture Principle,[5] *in 1966, you seemed to be acutely aware that something momentous was happening to the world, and you chose architecture to address this state of emergency: "We are on the threshold of an event," you wrote, "that has no historical precedent. We have already witnessed numerous transformations in society, but there never has been mutations of humanity itself. And yet we are confronted with the imminence of this metamorphosis."*

...I believe there has been a confirmation of this...

You were announcing a dizzying mutation of our relation to space capable of transforming immediate consciousness. This was the germ of what you developped later in terms of the global time of generalized interaction...

True, except when I said those things, I still was a spatialist. I thought that our relationship to the space of the world was without reference, that we had already reached globality. But it merely was a geographical, a geometric phenomenon: whence the "oblique function," whence topology (behind the oblique function there is topology), and whence geopolitics, I would say. I was already working on military space when I was writing on the bunkers. You had to believe it all went together. It was totally spatial. In this respect it lacked one dimension, and that dimension is time.

Let's stay with space for a moment. The "oblique function" you just alluded to, was a totally unheard-of architectural conception then since it was relying on inclined planes and no longer on vertical planes. How does the oblique function translate in topological terms?

It meant that there is no longer any inside and outside, only above and below. The topological system, the "oblique function," amounted to using oriented surfaces rather than ruled surfaces. That was the big revolution. From the beginning, orthogonal architecture has relied on ruled surfaces and ruled volumes, like the sphere, the pyramid, the parallelepiped, the cube. These surfaces are ruled by Aristotelian figures. The ruled surface is Euclid. In a post-Euclidian space, it goes without saying that surfaces are oriented.

The Space of War

How did you manage to move from geography to geopolitics? What got you interested in the bunkers and in military space in the first place?

22

My relationship to war. War was my starting point. I discovered the bunkers when I discovered freedom. During WWII I was in Nantes. It wasn't until after the Saint-Nazaire pocket fell into the hands of the Allies that I went for a swim at La Baule in a "micheline," a little car on rails that went to the sea. There I simultaneously discovered the deserted beach and those first blockhouses. I had never before seen those open structures, facing the emptiness, expressing the littoral dimension of total war. The aerial dimension I had already experienced in strategic bombing. For me the space of war was night-time alerts, and also hostages taken at night. I became interested in the space of war long before I ever thought of doing architecture. My discovery of the bunker was the discovery of a child who was claustrophobic—I also suffer from asthma. For me the bunker is a kind of metaphor for suffocation, asphyxiation, both what I fear and what fascinates me.

That's also the expressionist side of the bunker—fear, terror, suffocation within a block of concrete ... Edgar Allan Poe...

Yes, you can say that. But the bunkers weren't voluntarily expressionist. They became so for reasons that have to do with weaponry. Let me remind you that the thinnest concrete wall of a bunker is five feet thick, and twenty feet of concrete for the submarine foundations. If there is one place where you're scared, it's a bunker. It's not so much the density of the concrete itself that is frightening; it's the destructive power of the weapons used at the time. Concrete does nothing but translate the deadly power of contemporary weapons, tallboys, etc.[6]

What attracts you to the bunker is its monstrosity.

The bunker is so very heavy, so frightening, in other words, so terrifying and fascinating—sorry, but I love Goya, and I love Antonin Artaud—because it is the reverse figure of the destructive power of the twentieth century. Auschwitz, Hiroshima, both. That's why the bunker, to me, is the symbol of modern times. The bunker is at once the place where they would put you to death and where they would let the deported starve to death. I'm thinking of Geneviève de Gaulle, Charles de Gaulle's grand-niece. She was deported to Ravensbruck, but they didn't dare gas her. They put her in a bunker to die there of hunger and dehydration. The bunker is a kind of symbol of this century of concentration and elimination. I'll give you an example: the paint in the air-raid shelters, the *Luftchutstraum*. To avoid using electricity—you know that it will most likely be interrupted during a bombing—they painted the walls of the shelters with phosphorus. At first people flocked to them by the hundreds, and in the end they stopped going, preferring instead to die in the streets. Why? Because they were on top of one another, as in a subway. And now and again the fans would stop on account of the bombs falling. People would suffocate. And with this phosphorus light you literally had an image of Dante's *Inferno*. To me the bunker is total war.

It is not only a military image. It is also an image of the war waged on civilians—an anticipation of the post-war years when one could no longer tell war and peace apart.

In my view, the bunker is one of the architectural figures for the twentieth century. Its relationship to architecture, or to Corbusier, doesn't interest me that much. I am not a Corbusian. I don't like that culture. I love painting.

There are numerous aesthetic turnarounds in Le Corbusier's career, and you find as well in his work certain expressionist elements, like the use of untreated concrete and materials left visible, for example in the "Jaoul House" during the fifties or in the "La Tourette" monastery in Eveux, near Lyons, in 1960. Does that have anything to do with the bunkers as well? I noticed that some projects that you did with Claude Parent, like the Sainte-Bernadette-du-Banlay chapel in Nevers in 1966, built like a bunker, have sometimes been referred to as "structural brutalism." Would you agree with that?

Brutalism comes from England: it's the Smithsons. It is not associated with concrete at all, but with pulling out the insides, the guts of the building, like at the Pompidou Center in Paris. Bringing out all the pipes, displaying the supports, the structure, making a facade of the skeleton. Concrete would be more like Expressionism. It's something else altogether.

Brutalism then would be associated more with the young English architects who started Archigram in 1961, Cedric Price, Peter Cook, the Smithsons. Unlike you, though, they had faith in progress and were enthusiastic about technology and industrial development, which they tried to pursue openly in their work. They welcomed plug-in cities and assembly-line buildings. Unlike the French, they were short on theory and long in draughtsmanship...

In France, Archigram had their work showcased in the Pompidou Center, even if they were not the ones who built it. The Beaubourg Center—that's brutalism. Whereas what interests me first and foremost is the phenomenon of war.

Bunkers

Actually taking guts out is both architecture and war.

That's true. In fact Le Corbusier was inspired by the bunker and German Expressionism. Let me remind you that it was Corbusier who was put in charge of urbanism at La Pallice-La Rochelle after the war. La Rochelle had been protected, but the port of La Pallice was bombed because it had a small submarine base. It was still in working condition and Le Corbusier found his voice in this expressionism of concrete mass. The rounded forms of the Ronchamp chapel are patterned on the bunkers. Just look at what he did previously with the "Villa Savoye," or "Chandigarh." "La Tourette" itself has some of the features of a submarine. Erich Mendelsohn's "Einstein Tower" is a dynamic form, as they used to say, and you will find Mendelsohn in the bunker as well, for other reasons. If there's a historical affiliation, it derives from Expressionism and dynamism since the form of the bunker must be aerostatic. Some bunkers have a bombshell shape. Why? So when a bomb falls, it doesn't explode; it only ricochets. They put sand all around, and the bomb buries itself in it. Other bunkers have rounded angles, and the shell will slide off. This relation to fluidity is what interests me. It's a like a smooth pebble, except that here it's worn down prematurely in order to prevent the surface from stopping the bomb. Nothing to do originally with the history of modern architecture.

It's the logistical aspect of architecture that led you to question the history of architecture and the status of Euclidean space, and not formal preoccupations, as some people alleged. Was the Sainte-Bernadette-du-Banlay chapel that you built in Nevers with Claude Parent accused of formalism as well? It was so obviously inspired by the bunker.

Michel Vial, the Bishop of Nevers, happened to hold an open competition for the architecture of Sainte-Bernadette's chapel at the time. For me Nevers was *Hiroshima mon amour*, the film by Marguerite Duras. Bernadette Soubirous, this young girl, is behind the vision of the Virgin Mary at Lourdes in 1858. It is in Nevers, at the Dames-de-la-Charité, that Bernadette died. For the centennial of her death, they were going to build her a chapel and I was called on to compete. I drew architecture, I even started drawing the old forms, but I was not an architect. I am still not one, either. So I went straight to Claude Parent and I suggested that we do the competition. Parent had already built. He worked with Le Corbusier and participated in the "Espace Group" with André Bloc[7] And then I began to do this form I am drawing here for you. Why? Because Sainte-Bernadette is the grotto at Lourdes, it is the grotto at Massabielle, and Massabielle is a really unfitting place: it's the pigsty. Men would also take prostitutes there at night. That's where the Virgin Mary was about to appear, which perfectly fits my faith, moreover. She appears where danger grows, preceded by the prostitutes and the good thieves. It's all there. For me, this grotto is the bunker. So I thought: splendid, what you experienced in the bunker, you'll draw it right there.

You had already studied the bunkers.

Yes, I had done some layouts, I already had quite a few photos. I was in Dusseldorf to meet some friends, and I photographed the *Luftchutstraum*, the air-raid shelters, the *Flaktum*, the DCA towers, etc. As it happened, in Dusseldorf some neighborhoods still were in ruins, and a *Luftchutstraum* had been turned into a church. I went to mass in a bunker that is called the Church of the Holy Sacrament. Seeing a place like that Christianized, a place of terror, haunted by fear, that's what interested me. And so when I came back, I realized that in reality, nuclear terror had only just begun. Those were the days of the *Atomic Cafe*. Everyone was building bomb shelters. And I decided that the grotto at Lourdes was today's bomb shelter. It is the place of horrors, the place of great fear, the end of the world. So I drew inspiration from the bunker to do the job. I chose the shape of a heart, the double ventricles, split in two, cut down the middle, broken. One of them is the choir for communion, and the other the choir for confession, where one says: "I admit that I am a total bastard, *mea culpa*." What I admit, what you admit. You don't say: "I'm wonderful, I'm pure." Then, on the other hand, as soon as you realize that you're a bastard, at that moment, we can love one another. This is the whole question of Judeo-Christianity. Anyway, this was my interpretation. And, of course, the chapel is an absolute monstrosity. It scares everyone. There were two projects that signed for the competition, and they asked Monseignor Vial to decide: "The other project being considered," he told me, "is a small chapel with little angels, but there is so much hatred for your project, this pile of concrete, that I am going to choose it." And since we were the winners, we were going to have to build this thing. Of course, there were immediate protests, articles in the local paper: "They have no right to build the chapel of God as a bunker..." Now just for you to know: Sainte-Bernadette's chapel of Nevers is now classified as a historical monument.

The Oblique Function

And what did you do after that?

After that, I worked a lot on topology, on forms that are slanted. Architecture has always developed within forms that are ruled: the sphere, the cylinder, the cube, etc. However, ruled forms and surfaces are a kind of geometric academicism. There have been different periods of architecture, but the geometric formalism has remained. Most architects limit themselves to Euclidean forms: the orthogonal. They put needles on top of the towers, and this became the Gothic, or whatever you like. But my particular concern was to enter into topology, in other words, into non-Euclidean spaces, to use vague forms, including at the level of the floor.

Emphasizing the floor was quite a new element. It was taking the opposite view to vertical forms, even to extreme verticality, like New York. In Architecture Principe, *you called New York the "culmination of the second urban order." You considered then the possibility of a* third *urban order more fluid and continuous, since it would "combine mechanical and pedestrian circulation, mobilizing the habitat through the opening of transfer spaces ..."*

Hence the idea of living on inclined planes and of having furniture coming out of the floor. I did research on it with the "living ground," *le sol à vivre*. You pull out table, chairs, bed from an inclined place and you push it back when you're done with it. You can leave the furniture, too, if you want to set it up permanently. The idea is that the floor is both furniture and building. It is at once movable and stationary. The floor is the surface that contains the entire life of the house: encasements, furniture, television. TV is an object that you watch between your legs. You practically step on it. It's like a pool or an aquarium. As with planetary reality, it is the ground that contains life.

But the ground is slanted as well.

The inclined plane of Beaubourg is an aberration: it's continuous. What is interesting is *making waves*, and then you straighten out from time to time. We were not at all against the horizontal—that would be an aberration, the horizontal is a ground—we simply did not want the horizontal to be permanent. In the "oblique function," the structure is self-carrying, which means that there is only ground. The structure is everywhere, so surfaces multiply and at the same time they can communicate among them. In addition, these inclined surfaces are really good for solar energy. Solar energy works with angles, and we already had that in mind. There were maquettes built on the idea. It's a little like an airplane door.

You were inspired at the time by the airplane wing. Why?

Because everything is in it. You can take a walk in the wing. In airborne wings there are guys walking down the middle. It was this idea of a structure that contains everything.

You were pushing for a revolution in space, but it didn't take hold.

It was a revolution in architecture that architecture did not want. At the time the French were still Corbusians. And there wasn't much of this kind of thing, with the exception of Frederick Kiesler—he is the one who built the "Shrine of the Book" house in Jerusalem. The building was shaped like a bowl.

Dancing Staircase

Other more recent architects, like Bernard Tschumi, are now using inclined planes.

30

Tschumi was at the Ecole des Beaux-Arts in Paris when we were doing the "oblique function," and he drew inspiration from it. He also did the "Glass Video Gallery" in Groningen which is inclined in two axes. Now it's all over the place. We are witnessing something that is truly a postural, a choreographic revolution in architecture, something that has never taken place before, except for the staircase. The staircase was the great revolution in architecture. Palladio—I feel like saying the *miracle* of Palladio—the wonder is to have figured out how to make a dance out of a staircase. It is still debated because it revolves. Architecture becomes choreographic with the "oblique function." When you go to the Château de Chambord, you become a man from that time just by walking up and down the staircases. You hold your head up high. You see yourself wearing a magnificent hat and a sword. You become Cyrano de Bergerac. It's extraordinary. The staircase works your body like a ballet master, and the "oblique function" is the same. There were two precedents, and we adored them, obviously. First there was Frederic Kiesler and the "Endless House." He used to do theater. Let's not forget that the choreography of the "oblique function" comes from theatrical stage design. Architecture has always been related to stage design for the great architects. I am a man of the theater, whence the relationship I had with Heiner Müller, the great German playwright. When I was a kid I designed theatrical sets for Sartre's *The Flies,* and for Nicolas Bataille's *A Season in Hell,* an adaptation of Rimbaud for the Théâtre de Poche de Montparnasse. I did *Macbeth,* the decor and the masks, etc. So, there is Frederic Kiesler and also Frank Lloyd Wright. I take my hat off to Kiesler and to the Guggenheim Museum.

You say that the ground contains everything, but one could also say that everything keeps escaping from it. The oblique planes were not meant to occupy the ground. Moreover, this was a characteristic of the utopian architecture of the sixties, Constant's "New Babylone," Yona Friedman, Yves Klein... There was an elevation on piles, then the horizontal like a bridge and the traffic circulated below. Nature was up above on the roof. And there was also the subterranean occupancy. In Klein's work, the machines were below ground...

You're exactly right. Utudjian, whom I met, even had the idea for a subterranean urbanism capable of clearing the surface of the earth and protecting us from atomic war. One musn't forget that during this period terror had reached an equilibrium, and that this feeling of a total accident was not simply ecological: it was also military. There was the film *Atomic Cafe* and the English film by Peter Watkins, *The Bomb*. It is true that the ground-line tended to be forgotten at the time because it was threatened with destruction, with contamination, in the case of nuclear war, and also with saturation. There was a desire to give nature back its space so as not to deprive ourselves of any. So some went for above, like Friedman, Constant, and the "oblique function," and some went for below, like Utudjian. So, working on the bunkers as I did, and that wasn't by chance, you'll notice that I did not choose to bury myself.

At the same time, behind the "oblique function" there already was the idea that the planet was shrinking, so we had to maximize the use of space.

The non-orthogonal makes it possible to increase the volume and the capacity by a hundred-fold—I exaggerate a bit—for the same surface material. You just have to accept that there are no useless surfaces in the "oblique function." I will give you a simple example: you can fit twenty cigarettes in an orthogonal package. If you keep the same amount of material and reshape the package, you can fit forty cigarettes. Moving from the orthogonal to topology amounted to taking back the walls for living. Without any support, without the addition of any new material, one increases from thirty to ninety square feet for the same dwelling, because the walls are sloping and become accessible. There is only one dead angle—that's inevitable. But now there is no more inside and outside. You have sur-face and sub-face, but no more wall. Only the flies really have access to the sub-faces, but all the sur-faces are accessible.

A Catastrophe in Slow Motion

It is a more ecological architecture.

Yes, it's ecological because for the same price of original material, it costs only an angle. If you keep the right angle, then on the contrary, you lose the separation and you lose the surface of the wall. Except for hanging pictures, it's not a useful surface. If you calculate the angle on the inclined plane, you recover the walls as useful surfaces. The separation is made by the floor. The history of architecture is columns, capitols, Gothic roofs, etc. The floor is nothing. Now the floor becomes the determinant element in architecture—something it has never been.

You put horizontality first, but it didn't have to be the only point of reference.

In some cases the inclined planes can be the reference, but not in every case. Mind you, the horizontal plane remains, it is not negated. What is negated is the vertical. On the other hand, after a threshold of recovery, there is a certain diversity. You can follow one angle or another. It's a ground. At that time I was interested in geomorphology, syncline, anticline, everything that goes into geology. Those were the books I was reading then—today they would bore me to death—and I had noticed that there is practically nothing flat on the surface of the Earth. Nothing. There are many more inclined planes.

Verticality is in fact the height of artifice.

Oh, totally. The height. It's the Tower of Babel. We come back to the idea of the skyscraper: Babel is the great catastrophe. Two historical catastrophes in the Bible are total accidents: one is Babel, and the other is the Flood. It is not by chance that they are linked together.

New York is Babel. The Tower that challenges the sky...

And thus we were absolutely critical of New York. Oh yes, this is beautiful what Corbu said: "New York is a catastrophe in slow motion." Beautiful, a really beautiful phrase.[8] But we systematically opposed the Tower. The Tower is an aberration, whether six thousand or six hundred feet high.

You called New York "an agonizing giant..." Still, a tower is ecological as well. It doesn't clutter up the ground.

True, but unless men grow wings, there's no communication. Take the Tour Montparnasse, right next door. [*We are seated at the terrace of La Coupole, our familiar meeting place.*] When she was young, my daughter would go to the Tour Montparnasse every time she needed a short-term job. You are sure to find work there because no one wants to stay for too long: it's infernal. Every tower is infernal. You don't need a fire for that. You have to come down.

Towers are too tall for their own good. The "oblique function" is more grounded.

In oblique architecture, there is a relation to the fundamental, postural body. What I said back then was that until now architects have dealt with ergonomics, that is, Vitruvius, the Vitruvian man; Leonardo da Vinci's man—who by the way is now an ad for Manpower. The golden-section of Le Corbusier is ergonomic...

What is ergonomics exactly?

Ergonomics is proportions, the possibility of measuring all distances...

... in relation to the human body.

The body is the reference for proportions: the height of furniture, for example. With the "oblique function," the body is still ergonomic, but it becomes first and foremost a mass of weight. It has weight. We come back to one of my most important themes: gravity. The fact that the body has weight is a crucial element of architecture, whereas to this day it is worthless, nul and void. When boards are strong enough to support the body, weight does not exist.

Resistance of the Body

In a way, the function of the oblique is to make weight perceptible again, to give it back its gravity, its resistance...

And to work with gravity, with heaviness, the way a sailboat works with the wind. They are Galileo's inclined planes. As soon as you tilt planes, things go down and you change the relation with space. With the orthogonal plane, the flat plane, as in the entire history of architecture, there is no difference between making one movement or another. On an inclined plane, climbing and descending are radically different; but climbing diagonally or descending diagonally are different *again*; and walking laterally is different *as well*. Every dimension, every direction of space becomes a modification of the body.

There is resistance to the body, and resistance makes us aware of the body's existence.

You work with fatigue and not only with indifference. It's an architecture that is non-indifferent, that plays off disequilibrium. The model to be followed is the dancer. What puts us into a situation of disequilibrium is the inclined plane. We are always in the process of restructuring ourselves. Why is Palladio's stairway so wonderful? Because it is the place for body movements. Why did architecture decline? Because it gave up on the staircase with the escalator or the elevator, and all you have left is the floor—everything is smooth. Hence, with the "oblique function," the idea of working on slanted surfaces, Möbius strips, Klein bottles, etc. When I work on the "oblique function," the places I love most, for example, are those cylinders that are flared below and vertical above. They still had some of those in the fairs outside of Paris during the fifties—a circle and an oval made in wood, and then the floors. It's like the curve of a velodrome, just a vertical cylinder, and guys on motorcycles or on bicycles could drive straight up, round and round. To me they're like centrifuges. I never forgot it when I was young. Living in space is dance. There are dancers that dance on a vertical surface with ropes. To me, that's what architecture has to be. The model of architecture is Nietzsche's dancer. The model that I used to admire was the "interchange." But inclined planes are only used for automobiles. And I said then: what a disaster to make such beautiful forms for cars when we could make forms like the Guggenheim Museum. Everybody loves the Guggenheim, it's obvious. Everybody loves the ramplike construction of Frederick Kiesler's "Endless House." Why? Precisely because it's the dancer. That's the logic we adhered to. We were not Corbusians.

In your manifestos, you and Parent were opposed to the automobile, and you were opposed to speed as well, which you considered dead time: "We want nothing to do with this proposition which is based on speed. We reject this idea. The exploration of space is crippling and renders the notion of speed old-fashioned. In the latest urban agglomerations, speed will no longer be considered a fundamental factor: it will no longer exist. Consequently, aerodynamism is going to crumble." Back then you really thought that we could resist speed?

That was a critique of automobile mobility. It dates back to the time when the model for the house was the car, even in Corbu.

Walking City

The car versus the highways...

Right, the highways. The car is also a form of mobility that was going to inspire the English Archigram's "Walking City." That's how you get the inverse concept of inhabitable circulation, and not mobile architecture. At the time, the conflict was between mobile architecture (a lot of people got behind it, it included aggregations of vehicles that formed buildings) and inhabitable circulation. And it is circulation which was to become inhabitable, and not mobile architecture. We come back full circle to topology, choreography, and the return to the body. In a car the body is dead, and I still hold to this critique.

Given the chance, what kind of architecture would you have made at the time?

I would have made experimental houses. What's important in architecture is housing. However, we could never get off the ground—there were no customers.

What about the "Mariotti House" that you mentioned in your book?

Mariotti was our building contractor. Like all contractors, he was loaded. He had bought some golf course at St. Nom-la-Bretêche—beautiful property. He knew that by owning a beautiful property not far from Paris and building such a house he would get publicity (eventually he got the magazine *Paris-Match* to cover it). We got the plan from him. He wanted I don't remember how many square feet, and we doubled his surface area. We built a maquette for him. He approved it. We went as far as the surveying. We were just deciding where to put the foundations, but his wife opposed the project. She was afraid to live on inclined planes. So from that point on, we realized that we couldn't get anything built. We were stigmatized. Construction was prohibited. They thought we were jokers. Sainte-Bernadette's chapel—everyone was against it, including the *Cahiers d'art sacré*. So there was no more work for us.

Couldn't you have built something other than an "oblique function" house?

The oblique is the only thing that really interested me. I had no desire to make money putting up orthogonal buildings.

But a good part of your work at the time was architectural research. Couldn't you have continued to do that?

I would have liked to continue the "oblique function." With the republication of the anthology, I read all the texts over again, and I was surprised to see that everything works. Archi-Principe didn't last very long: 1963 to 1968. Five years, a flash. It was too short-lived. But the "oblique function" is a theory that works quite well. It was like an engine in neutral, it just needed an intelligence to put it in gear. I am surprised to see behind the Greg Lynns, the Marcus Novaks, the Lars Spuybroeks, that the younger generation has rediscovered it with the computer, since it is easier now to calculate the forms. We used to build maquettes. You can still take it up today, with modifications obviously, but I mean it is inevitable in the future—I am totally convinced of it, this is not prophecy—one day we will see completely oblique houses.

You did some experiments to test the resistance of the body to inclined planes. And there is not just one kind of resistance either. There are all sorts of resistances.

All sorts. But since the gradation was quite well calculated—we did the "Pendular Destabilizer" under medical observation—there was clearly something pleasant about it. It was not constraining.

You were ready to start the experiment in 1968. Instead it was the "events" of May that took off...

Yes. And we were supposed to conduct this experiment at the University of Nanterre...

Entering Space-Time

... Nanterre, that's where it all began! So the experiment got destabilized in other ways. What did it consist of?

I knew some doctors, and I told them: we have to do it full-scale and lock ourselves up in a structure with electrodes to monitor the behavioral consequences of living in it over the course of a month ...

It was like an experiment in a zero gravity ...

Zero gravity, disequilibrium. In order to adjust still further our understanding of inclined planes. The advantage of the oblique is that you can choose what you want, whereas with the orthogonal, or with Le Corbusier, the right angle is always straight and up. Architecture Principe was based on breaking the orthogonal in every way. It no longer accepted the tyranny of the right angle. Entering into topology—you can say into "the fold," even if Gilles Deleuze had not yet written his essay on the baroque at the time—we did a lot of work on it. We had a lot of choices to play with, but they were dependent on the experiment. We had wooden structures, and we were going to live on top of them ...

It's like the fair you mentioned earlier. Were they temporary structures?

Yes. They were suspended up there.

And what kind of model did you have in mind?

The Circadian rhythms.[9] The relationship to time, which is linked to the twenty-four-hour cycle. When I was getting the "Pendular Destabilizer No. 1" ready, I had in mind Michel Siffre and his speological experiments as a way of living "beyond time." Do you remember Siffre and his cave?

He is the man who remained in the dark some four-hundred fifty feet underground for two months in the south of France, only connected to the outside world by radio. He was testing down there extended stays in bomb shelters or onboard artificial satellites. These were the preoccupations of the period. As he drily said in his book, Beyond Time,[10] *"humans first sheltered in caves, and in this century of progress it looks as though they might end up back there."*

Siffre wanted to show that in a situation of absolute confinement, when there was no way of discriminating between night and day —through light, heat, etc.—one would totally lose all temporal references, and therefore experience time in a way that was not human—an infra-meteorogical or infra-physiological time affecting every vital cycle. First Siffre worked in a laboratory in Lyon, then he went to the United States and experimented with time changes, trying to understand what kind of future there was in these rythms. In this respect he anticipated the essay Henri Lefèbvre wrote much later on "rhythmanalysis." You can't develop a non-Euclidean architecture unless you enter into space-time.

And that's what the "Pendular Destabilizer No. 1" was for?

Siffre's experiments interested us because it was a research on time that we had not envisaged ourselves. Hence the idea of experimenting time and space. We were going to lock ourselves up in Nanterre, close to the campus where May '68 was just about to explode, not far either from the new La Defense district where we had contacts with a few urban specialists. Our cave was an "oblique function" kind of contraption with inclined planes, each one different from the other, so that we could experiment with them—a systeme of inclines and then a threshhold of re-equilibration, an other system of inclines, etc.

The system of inclines is somewhat ondulatory?

Yes. When I say system, I mean angulation. All angles were different in relation to the horizontal. In order to test them, you had to have several of them, and then you chose what seemed to work best. All this was done with electrodes, with medical supervision. And we were due to lock ourselves up in there in 1968. Our goal was to test living on the inclined planes and examine the behavioral changes, not in relation to time, but in relation to equilibrium. Because the relation of movement to the ponderal mass is connected to gravity, and there wasn't any test available in that area. Everyone knew about gravity in water, or in a centrifuge (at the time there was a lot of interest in space travel), so we decided to have a "centrifuge" to study inclines. Which ones? There were not that many because when one climbs beyond a certain angle, then it become a moot point. Below, there are all kinds of inclines, like those devised for the handicapped. So we identified a sytem of inclines and we built them in the "destabilizer."

These inclines created a resistance short of provoking a fall.

Yes, and then you identified the inclines that were the more agreable by testing them on the body.

And all this was meant to be entered into a architectural program.

We had to build the "Mariotti House" and that would have been very helpful. We couldn't just hand out plans merely tested with three boards and climing on top of them to see if it felt good or not. We had to live *inside it*, figure out if the system of re-balancing had to be widened or reduced, etc. Climbers know about these kinds of experiments and we had contacts with them as well. They are used to live in unusual situations, like hanging a sleeping bag on top of a cliff... Everything was ready, and then nothing happened, it ended right there. I know that my collegue was a bit worried that we would be ridiculed publicly. People didn't believe in it, the two of us trapped like rats in a laboratory with medical supervision à la Siffre. And Siffre was far away, no one could get to him. And then he was dealing with physiology, and we were dealing with architecture. Claude Parent wasn't very eager to commit to this experiment, and he was relieved when it was dropped. I deeply regretted it myself. We had been looking for extreme situations, like this other Frenchman who crossed by foot the great American desert, experimental situations for the body. I am not talking about auto-mutilation, obviously, just attempts to push the body to the limit. It was a bit like competition. There was a sport-like dimension to our research, that's for sure.

Experimental, sportive et existential all at the same time..

Yes, not to forget the electrodes. This is something that should exist more in architecture anyway, tests.

There's no simulation for this kind of gravity, as they do for space travel?

Practically none. South of Paris there were a few experimental architects we would have loved to work with, but they didn't take our project seriously. Architectural experiments—on proportions, lights, etc.—are few and far between. There is a ready-made "knowledge" people rely on… And then they believe that it works as long as it is orthogonal. But it is not true. They hight of ceilings, for instance, could be very disquieting. At the time I went to see Dr. Sivadon, a psychiatrist, at the Marcel-Rivière Institute, even invited him to talk at the Ecole Spéciale d'Architecture. Remarkably intelligent man. Do you know about him?

Yes. He became Head-Psychiatrist at the Ville-Evrard hospital near Paris in 1943, the year Antonin Artaud left it for the Pereire asylum in Rodez. Sivadon's sister had been deported to Ravensbruck and he quickly realized that nothing looked more like a death camp than Ville-Evrard. He tried to change that and he was among those few who set out to renovate French psychiatry after the war.

Dr. Sivadon was passionate about the "oblique function" and we spent the day with him and a few mad people there, some of them apparently quite dangerous. There was a padded room with some of them literally climbing the walls… They certainly didn't need inclined planes. At lunch there was a woman patient who said that she couldn't bear eating in the dining-room because the ceilings were too high. And I understand that very well, being claustrophobic myself, just the reverse. That's why I always go seat at La Coupole, where the ceilings are very high. At that time in France you could meet everybody, there was an intense inter-communication that has disappeared since. That's how I met David Cooper and Félix Guattari (through Deleuze). When you told people that you were an architect they didn't laugh at you then. As for the architects themselves, they couldn't believe we had paid a visit to a madhouse. They still were into Le Corbusier. Anyway all this is gone. Now everyone is back in their little compartments.

2. DROMOLOGY

May 1968 □ Urban Revolutions □ Rhythmic Discordance □ Escape Velocity □ Concentration of Distances □ Political Economy of Speed □ Two Spaces □ Polar Inertia □ Standardization/Synchronization □ Temporal Compression □ Grey Ecology □ Critical Space □ Portable-Self □ Architecture of Feedback □ Tele-Presence □ Escape from Humanity

I'm sure May 1968 destabilized all that. It managed to destabilize the entire country, and your own pendular destabilizer to boot. Earlier on you mentioned that you had moved from space to time, but you didn't say how you made this transition—if there was one, of course, because it was such a sudden leap. Was May '68 a big factor, or a helpful accident?

That's a good question. And it's also a historical one. Because it happens that I was involved in a fundamental way in the events of '68. You know that already. It's been recorded in the histories of the

May '68 period: when I took the Odéon Theater in Paris with Jean-Jaques Lebel, with Julian Beck and the people from Living Theater, *I passed into history*. Now I don't mean, of course, that I have become a historical figure. Not at all. I mean that I moved into time. Up to that point I had worked on topology, on the notion of oblique space, the fact of going beyond orthogonality, everything which is exploding today thanks to computer technology—it's complex space in the manner of Frank Gehry and others—I was wrapped up in that stuff, and the question of time did not exist, even if I had some feeling for time through relativity, the space-time continuum. In Architecture Principe, the question of geometry remained central. Space was the essential thing. But we were basically on the verge of converting space-time into space-speed. Then bang! I suddenly found myself standing in history, in time, because the events of '68 are temporary-temporal events. They are events, and they must remain events, by which I mean ephemeral.

Time was already present in war.

Yes. My work on speed has its beginnings in the war, *Blitzkrieg*, the political importance of speed, speed and politics, but also in the relativity of space. You can't construct space without constructing time, without raising the question of the use of time and the use of space. From there I broke off from architecture because architects are too formalist and it takes too long for them to build. They make too much money, and they cut themselves off.

May '68

May '68 was also a big blow to French architects. It exploded the hierarchical structure of the profession. Until then it was still rigidly organized along medieval lines, like a guild, with masters and apprentices. Architecture students were not even considered students. No wonder it was more of a liberating event for them. Some of them went pretty far, just like you…

Yes, it had an impact on everybody. An entire generation was affected by it. As for the architects themselves, let's just say that it was the end. The postwar reconstruction was not yet quite over at the time—there still were some enormous construction sites—but there was no competition. Young architects were the servants of the company bosses. They didn't stand a chance, and that's why we had such costly journals, why we constructed maquettes, why they called us "paper architects." But we met a ton of people in those days. We met Paolo Soleri, Walter Pichler, Buckminster Fuller. In Folkstone we met the Archigram people. The cat was out of the bag, and there were enormous hopes. Parent and I went our separate ways in May '68. He was against it, I was for it. He went to the right, and I went to the left. My origins are in the working-class districts, the Communist Party. I'm a leftist. Leftism, the movement of '68, I'm all for it, even if I'm slightly anomic—not at all Marxist or Maoist, but more on the side of the anarchists. Those two worlds were side by side but didn't see one another. There were the red flags, there were the black flags. I marched with the black flags, until one day I pulled out a transparent flag, an anomist flag, the "anomist movement" which I created with a piece of clear plastic. [*Laughs*] They also published a recording on which I declaim the manifesto of the anomist movement. Black—its past bugged me. There was too much black. It was always the same.

You're still wearing black all the time. Is it the anarchist or the priest?

If there were no other flags around, I would move in with the black flags. Anarchist-Christian. And you know I haven't changed. That's how we found one other, too—huh, Sylvère? The idea was to express all of this in a public place, and that was the Odéon Theater. When we took it over, there were all sorts of theater people there, actress Delphine Seyrig, etc.; all the actors came to join us. And of course the people of the French Happenings, the Living Theater. (Jean-Louis Barrault had invited them to the Odéon and they sided with the students who seized the auditorium, which put him in an impossible situation.) As if by accident we found ourselves mixed up with theater people, but it was pretty logical. The relation to the body in the "oblique function" is the dancer, the actor. It wasn't academic. We wound up with them in '68—and then it was cut off. Students came to hear me speak at the Odéon, and they ended up asking me to teach at the Ecole Spéciale d'Architecture on Boulevard Raspail in Paris—one of the two professors that they invited to pursue their career there—and not building much of anything, I wound up teaching and then doing theory.

You ended up doing theory for lack of anything better...

I went to the Ecole Spéciale d'Architecture, so I wound up cut off from my base, in the terrestrial sense of the word. The "oblique function" was meant to give the greatest value to the latest element, the ground, that had not been highlighted. Necessarily, from that moment on, I was cut off from architecture, in the sense of architectural research. After that, I could no longer work on space, except outside of teaching. I cut myself off from my roots, I became a man of words, and what's more I was involved in a political movement. There you have it: a historical soldering—May '68 passed through.

Passed through like an angel ... but it was an earthquake. It could also have ended up badly.

You remember Grimaud, the Prefect of Police, both a scholar and a poet, marvelous guy—he tells the story that when the kids who were marching shouted Situationist sentences at him, he didn't react in the least. "For me," he wrote in his *Memoirs*, "May '68 was the last great literary revolution in Europe." It was not a political happening like the October Revolution, or 1789, it was a literary event. I totally agree with him. That's the side I was on. So, in a way, I was happy I ended up teaching. It kept me from selling floors. As for Parent, he ended up building nuclear reactors, which I would never have agreed to do. So that's where we really split up.

You got involved with time by getting involved with your own time.

From then on, it was obvious to me that I was going to work on the notion of time, and thus on phenomena of acceleration, of movement. These were already prefigured by inhabitable circulation: the big theme of topology was to make circulation inhabitable, and no longer to inhabit only what is stationary. (The stable aspect of what is stationary goes a long way to explain verticality, orthogonality, the right angle, etc.) I was going to wind up studying dynamics, and also historical dynamics, in other words, the city. And I was going to develop things on the city. To that point, I had written texts on architecture (in Bloc's *Architecture Aujourd'hui*, in *Architecture Principe*). There was architecture, but of course I had already written on the American riots, which were in a way similar to what the Situationists were doing around that time. Now I was definitely involved in the history of the city...

Urban Revolutions

What interested you about the American riots?

I was convinced that the Watts riots, the Detroit riots, or those in Newark were the beginning of an urban revolution. I thought that the next war was going to be a war of cities. I wasn't thinking about the oppositions among minorities; I thought the city had become unlivable, the opposite of what it should be, i.e. a place of socialization. On the contrary, I believed that the city de-socialized and the Americain riots were the beginning of an urban revolution. I was using the term, too, long before Henri Lefèbvre ever used it. I also believed that the urban revolution was actually under way, but differently, with a multi-ethnic dimension. The recent riots in Los Angeles were repressed by troops like those coming back from the war with Iraq, and who took care of the urban revolution. What is happening right now all over France is of the same nature. The suburbs are on the verge of a civil war—a civil war of cities, not a civil war of nations. A "sporadic" civil war, as they say, which is no longer located in time, as the Spanish Civil War was located in time. I already said as much in 1966, in *Architecture Principe*. And I hope there will be an outcry for a different city, a different life. Remember that I worked with Anatole Kopp, who published *City and Revolution*.

At the time you had also considered the idea of going beyond the city...

Yes, the idea of evacuating cities in cases of extreme pollution. It's an extraordinary thing to evacuate cities independently of a state of war...

What happened to Phnom Penh already *was pretty eerie: city dwellers massacred or thrown out in the countryside, entire districts replaced by rice fields, their own population considered "prisoner of war" by the Khmer leaders...*

Yeah, another Cambodia was in the offing: Phnom Penh and Angkar [the Khmers Rouges shadow organization]. In fact, Phnom Penh grabbed the attention of utopianists. I knew many friends who thought then that it was great. They would say: "Finally, it's happening." Not me, I must say. I'm not Marxist enough for that. I wasn't Marxist at all, and I confess, seeing Phnom Penh emptied on television terrified me. I was the one who had worked on the idea of abandonning cities... This military dimension did not correspond in the least with the ecological dimension which was my own. The "oblique function," by the way, is also ecological. It's about preserving the lithospheric texture, as I have said. At that time no one was really talking about ecology yet. In the States, yes, but not in France. Only after '68 will it be brought up. Then you had notions like the hydropshere, the lithosphere, the atmosphere: this is something I am concerned about. My vision is an aerialized vision.

Cities as you saw them weren't meant to be emptied, just streamlined. In Speed and Politics,[11] *you defined cities in terms of circulation, a city street being only a crossroad ...*

Yes. The city has multiple speeds, like a gearshift, with a clutch to engage and disengage. So I was going over completely to the city, war (war and technology are linked in my opinion), and technological progress—well, "progress" is in quotation marks. This led to *L'Insécurité du territoire*[12] [The Insecurity of the Territory] and *Speed and Politics* in 1966 and 1977.

And that completely changed your point of view...

Oh, completely. Completely. From the moment I started working on speed, I never again worked on geometry, even if I kept refering to tele-topology, which is the topology of rays and wave emissions. I have given some examples of it, the video surveillance of a building, for instance: when you can see the totality of the building in each room, you are in a Klein's bottle, but on a topological level. On the other hand, if you take the geometry of an orthogonal building, and in each room you can see the totality of the building, then space turns back on itself, which is what I call "tele-topological." I talk about it in *Lost Dimension* [*L'Espace critique*],[13] it goes way back. It's the first book I did that makes the connection between the two, between the dimension in which geometry dominates—geometry coupled with national and regional development—and the other dimension in which time is urban development. All the way to the world-city, where the territory becomes world thanks to the tele-cam, thanks to tele-action, etc. But history passed through the middle of it: the event of '68.

The event projected you into tele-action...

I didn't choose it. Most likely, if I had continued on after Nevers, after the "Mariotti House," I would have stayed with the notion of an oblique habitation, with the tele-topo-lodging, "home sweet home."

The inclined plane became the springboard to another career...

I have written practically nothing on architecture after that, aside from a few short articles, and a bit in *Lost Dimension*, too, which resulted from a research contract I had with the Ecole Spéciale. Architecture was diverted into teaching.

Le Corbusier never interested you in terms of architecture. Was there anyone else you ever cared for?

I was interested in Hans Scharoun, who did the Berlin Philharmonic but also some really astonishing housing in Siemenstadt. I went to Germany, my very first trip, to meet him. Had I had a mentor in architecture—I never did have one since I came to it in a roundabout way, through the bunkers—it would have been Scharoun. A very graphic, baroque man. But I quickly broke with all that ... Why? Because I entered into topology.

Rhythmic Discordance

Henri Lefèbvre was very involved with architecture in urban terms, meaning that, just like you, he thought it was a reality in crisis. Was he interested in your work in any way?

No. Actually he was very opposed to it. He was totally against us at the time of Architecture Principe, and he didn't hesitate to make fun of us. As for us, we more or less admired *La Révolution urbaine* [The Urban Revolution][14] because he was venturing into our territory.

His Critique of Everyday Life[15] *had already raised the question of time.*

Yes. Moreover, with the posthumous publication of his last book, *Eléments de Rythmanalyse* [Elements of rhythmanalysis],[16] he and I were in agreement. It's a small, unfinished work.

It's quite interesting the way he analyses urban rhythms in their plurality, their association and interaction, their relation to space, inner space as well as outer space. And their destiny too, since they oscillate between polyrhythmy and arhythmy (implosion, explosion). The term rhythmanalysis *is borrowed from Gaston Bachelard, who started elaborating on* durées *and rhythmic discordance...*

Yes, but Lefèbvre was moving toward "dromology."[17] From the moment you speak of rhythmology, you introduce the question of speed. Not merely biological rhythms, but sociological rhythms, acceleration. And Lefèbvre understood this by reading *Lost Dimension.*

In Architecture Principe *you hadn't yet found that dimension.*

No, the notion of time was missing; I am perfectly aware that we blew it. I remember telling Claude Parent: this book by Lefèbvre deals with a dimension that we don't.

How did you end up coming to an understanding with Lefèbvre?

One day I got a telephone call from him, and he said: "I would like to spend an evening with you at Renaudie's house." Jean Renaudie was one of the good French architects, I would say the only good one of his day ... Him and his wife, Gailhoustet, were very close to the Communist Party. Renaudie was already dead by then. So I spent an evening with Lefèbvre and Renaudie's son, also an architect—he built the Ivry suburb for the C. P. Lefèbvre already was very old, it was a few months before his death. I remember him as I remember Deleuze at the end of his life. We were sitting down, and Lefèbvre said, "Ah, Paul, you and I have

55

had our disputes." It's true. We didn't get along, he was one of my enemies—all those "liberals" we didn't see much of in 1968, as usual. Anyway I said, "Yes, we don't always see eye to eye."

What were his main objections?

He too thought my work was formalist. He didn't really get it, but I have to admit that it might look that way. And he said: "I am glad to see you again because I read *Lost Dimension*." The book had just come out [in 1984]. And he said: "I really loved the book. I understand now what you're trying to do, and I'm very interested." I really wanted to tell him: that's because, at some point, you told us yourself: "Before space there is time." It was in 1963 or '64, at that time I had not yet thought of speed. And it is true that I started working on the notion of time because it seemed an element that had been left aside. And Lefèbvre added: "I am also putting together a book on 'rhythmology.'" In a way, rhythmology draws on my work. Not that Lefèbvre needed to draw inspiration from me. He didn't do dromology. But he himself said: "You know, Paul..." His book appeared posthumously, and people don't discuss it enough. I bring it up a lot because it's a really important book.

Escape Velocity

How important is it for you?

It went into what we were introducing with the notion of dromology through an intelligence of politics that is choreographic. The idea of rhythmology belongs to the political economy of speed, and when I talk about speed, I am talking about bodies, and not about vehicles. Vehicles are just scooters, even if it's a jet. I am interested in the body as the central object of political space. What is essential is the relation of speed to the body in the political rhythm, and the city is the place, the gearbox, or it should be the gearbox of the political economy of speed, and not only the political economy of wealth and capital.[18] What I am telling you now is incontrovertible. I'm not trying to brag about it. I mean, it is incontestable. We've already arrived, and it's where we're headed. The political economy of speed is becoming an absolute necessity. It is not simply an ecological problem: there is an ecology of time just like there is an ecology of space. The idea of the pollution of distances in nature is also an architect's idea. We come back to ergonomics: the world is on a human scale. Imagine that a human being were not six feet tall, but sixty feet tall: the Earth becomes uninhabitable. The architect works with ergonomic proportions, with masses that have weight. We talked about these things in relation to the "oblique function," but this is a major political question. It is not simply an architectural problem. It is a problem of globalization.

You were already touching on this question in Architecture Principe.

Of course, I talked about it. But my approach was too metaphorical. I realized from the beginning that the dimension of time was getting away from us, but I couldn't do more because I had not entered into it. I was totally in topology. Time had not been dealt with, even if there were references to speed and to choreography. And yet I was really interested in the question of the space-time continuum—especially since I continued to have an approach that was critical of military questions: the question of time had become central with Euromissiles and satellites armed with nuclear weapons. With the Euromissiles, we were getting closer to the point where war would become automatic. I even called that: the *automatic response*. It's "Dr. Folamour."

There was no more time to make a decision.

When they moved the Euromissiles closer, we were back to 1962 with the Cuban affair. What was most threatening with the Cuban affair is that the Russians had brought the missiles closer and reduced the time for response. As long as the Euromissiles had to cross the Atlantic, there was still time for the big radars in Canada and elsewhere to spot them. But not from Cuba, and they had to be destroyed at any cost, risking a nuclear war. In the 70s, with the Euromissiles, it was down to a matter of minutes on both sides. That was the time André Glucksman, Yves Montand and the other French intellectuals were demonstrating in the streets, shouting: "Better be Red than Dead."

Deterrence actually meant hijacking entire populations through a nerve game and it could have got out of hand at any time.

The phenomenon of deterrence is something that dominated our lives, but no one has really analyzed it. It was analyzed in terms of game theory, the games of deterrence played between Russians and Americans, but strangely enough it is not something that has been analyzed philosophically. When the Berlin Wall collapsed, I thought, Well, if there is a book that needs to be written now, it is "The Deterred," but it would take another Dostoievsky to write it the way he wrote *The Possessed*. And I truly believe that towards the end of the twentieth century we have all been "deterred" and there was nothing anyone could do about it. We have experienced an end of art, or an end of politics that was soft enough, because there still was some kind of end. But with the breakdown of deterrence we experienced the end of a "soft" world and I can't even talk about it myself anymore. In some strange way, my intelligence of deterrence is gone. It's just a word now.

The disappearance of deterrence was another casualty of the Cold War, the war that never happened except in its effects.

Something escaped. We were steeped in it, and suddenly…

… it was gone.

Vanished, and we didn't derive anything from it, except that now deterrence is everywhere. It is not just buried in the nuclear silos of the Albion plateau or under the Rocky Mountains, it is everywhere.

In a sense, deterrence has replaced life itself.

Exactly. The globalization of liberalism is a deterrence of politics.

Everything at this point is going too fast to settle into anything. The Cold War didn't rely yet on this instantaneity of time, although time was becoming the crucial factor. This opened up the space-time dimension.

We had entered relativity. Not just Einstein's and his incomprehensible formulas: we were beginning to experience instantaneity through the speed of light, with the lasers. Star Wars would soon follow suite.

It was not just time: space itself was in the process of mutating and becoming planetary. You spoke then about a "feeling of liberation," but escape velocity *did not yet exist.*[19] *The thrust towards outer-space, its conquest, was just beginning.*

True, but it interested me at the time. I saw the first Sputnik when I was a kid. I was already very aware that the conquest of space was a radical break, causing the loss of our bodies. I thought, we can't lose the Earth. And I continue to believe the same thing.

You did not want to forget "the rugged reality to be embraced..." [Rimbaud].

It was necessary to give back to the Earth a sense which it had lost with the second urban order, the vertical order, a sense it had lost with the Babelization of the city, of every city, New York being one example. Babelization today is Shanghai, Hong Kong.

You used to depict New York almost as a rocket ready to take off.

The vision I had at the time was spatialist and aerial, as if the city were taking off from the ground to free it up, restoring it to its original nature. The oblique planes were intended not to occupy the ground. Just look at my drawings: my visions were aerial. Also, in "Nautacity," there were men flying around with rocket-packs. So there was an idea that urbanism was becoming aerial.

But in the case of New York, you felt that there was something diabolical about this elevation...

Yes. I was against what was going to become the New Age, or Heaven's Gate. I was against the negation of the Earth. And I am still against it. I was in favor of the conquest of space, but against those who want to abandon the Earth and deny that the one is neccesary to the other. That explains my interest in Heaven's Gate. In subsequent books I said it was crazy. Yes, in my view, the New Age and Heaven's Gate are connected.

Pushed to the limit, the New Age becomes suicidal.

Go beyond escape velocity, and it's boom! It's not the rocket, either. But the real myth is outer-space: look at the zero-gravity cemeteries that they are now sending up into orbit.

Timothy Leary is the most recent recruit. Everyone can see him circling round and round the earth, his last acid trip...

There you have a kind of idealization of space, and I don't care for it either in the least. The "oblique function" gave the greatest architectural value to the last element, the ground, that had never been highlighted. Up to that point, it was where you spit, where you put sawdust. I would say that the ground is the feminine.[20]

If in the beginning the Earth was the mother, then the orthogonal would be an erection. It sounds pretty Oedipal...

You could say that the "oblique function" goes beyond the erection. Topology is the consequence of the ground coming into history. Suddenly the ground becomes general. There is now only the ground [*sol*] and the *entresol* [mezzanine]. The inside and the outside are no longer connected. It's a Klein bottle. In effect, the relation with space becomes feminized, a dynamic of fluids, something we were going to discuss a great deal afterwards, including women's struggles, which I am passionate about. This has always been the case in architecture: the grotto, the womb... I touched on it, too, when I said woman was the first vehicle of humankind.[21]

Contraction of Distances

In Architecture Principe *Claude Parent wrote: "By achieving general mobility within the habitation, the oblique will transform the old cells which are nothing but micro-ghettos... Everything that is erected between man and movement is going to disappear." With the "oblique function," the womb is no longer compartmentalized. The body is everywhere.*

Perhaps this has to do with the fact that I am a Christian. Here we come back to the incarnation, we discover *incarnatus*. Not the resurrection, but the incarnation converted me. And if it is not *incarnatus*, it is a monstrosity. So I am opposed not only to fascism, as many people are, thank God, but also to eugenics, and still more to the traffic in genetics which is in the works for the human genome. This is very important: the body is central, and each catastrophe is an initiation. The catastrophe of the Titanic invented the "Soul." Save Our Souls, SOS. Given catastrophes today, like genetics, now it's Save Our Bodies. How would you say it in English...

(Laughs) Well, it would be SOB... Do you know what this means in English?

No.

Son of a Bitch.

You're kidding. (*He slaps his thigh.*) This is perfect.

And now we would have to say: Save Our Planet. Space is shriveling up now in favor of time, and time belongs to no one. The world is no longer on a world scale.

We are confronted with the phenomenon of confinement. Michel Foucault analyzed the great imprisonment in the eighteenth century with the closing of asylums, the disciplinary politics of the Great Enclosure. But the Great Enclosure isn't behind us with Bentham's *Panopticon*, it is ahead of us with globalization. And I would say that this is the *grey* ecology. Besides the ecology of substances, the green ecology, there is an ecology of distances. The telluric contraction of distances, the *pollution of distances*, as I call it—not the pollution of nature but the pollution of distances in nature—this will make the Earth uninhabitable. People will suffer from claustrophobia on the Earth, in the immensity of the planet.

I can go to La Rochelle for thirty dollars round trip with my senior citizen card. [*Virilio just moved from Paris to La Rochelle, an old fortified harbor on the Atlantic coast*]. But tomorrow we will go to Montreal or Tokyo for three dollars, for nothing. And then? How far can we go? That's what I always say: to what point? When are we going to understand the notion of closure? The world is limitless? No. It is increasingly closed and contracted. In a sense, these places will all equal nothing. Incarceration will become a mass phenomenon, an apocalyptic phenomenon.

In fact, we will no longer feel like traveling. Howard Hughes won't be the only one: people will experience "polar inertia" on a mass scale.[22]

You go for a walk by the sea, and on the beach you watch the waves, as in "The Day After," not a bad film, either. Except, now, the last shore is not the atomic bomb, it's the *dromic* bomb, it's the contraction of the world. *The bomb does not explode, the world implodes.* The day is not far off—just a few generations, or so they say—when the world will be reduced to nothing, both on the level of telecommunications and on the level of supersonic transportation. Then the world will implode in the soul of humanity. They will be totally trapped, totally asphyxiated by the smallness of the world on account of time and speed. This has nothing to do with demographics. They once thought that the world would be unlivable because there would be billions and billions of people. Before we get to that point, it will become uninhabitable from speed, from pollution.

This explains the urgency to get back to the body, to the scale of nature, as long as they exist...

What would be needed is a political economy of speed that refers to sensations. The political economy of wealth—it concerns the Physiocrats. It's Quesnais. Who was François Quesnais? He was a doctor, a man interested in bodies and their pathologies, their sensations.[23] And it is my belief that today we have given up on all that. Sensations today are virtual reality, cassettes, robots. But perceptual sensations, *politically* perceptual sensations, those of the masses—not simply those of the individual—it is a field that has been left totally fallow. They want to get rid of humanity to replace it with Supermen...

In Architecture Principe, *you wrote: "Consciousness must be awakened by the absolute, inescapable necessity of slowing down the rhythm of architecture to keep it from following the acceleration of the human mutation." This isn't only true of architecture.*

That is the role of the brake. Architecture is a brake, but in a positive sense. Ten years ago I did this big exhibit on speed at Cartier, in Jouy-en-Josace, and what image did I use at first? The Pharaoh. Why? Deleuze and I discussed it quite a bit. What is the Pharaoh? The two hands crossed on his chest are holding, on the one side, a hook, and, on the other, a whip. According to Egyptologists, the whip is a fly-chaser. I said: You've got to be joking. Think of a chariot: there is a hook to pull the reins, and a whip to accelerate. What the Pharaoh possesses is the power of the Pontif, the one who directs energies. The hook is wisdom, it's the brake. It is also the Pope's hook or the Bishop's cross. Then, on the other side, you have the fly-chaser? I'm sorry, things like that drive me crazy. The whip no one discusses anymore is Ceausescu, the *conducator.* Except today we don't have a whip anymore, we have a pedal. So this is the idea: there will be no truly philosophical politics, I mean, any political philosophy other than barbarism if we don't control speed the way we monitor wealth, if economy is not extended to time, since time is money and speed is power.

Political Economy of Speed

Fluidity is not synonymous with speed, on the contrary. Speed pushes towards abstraction whereas fluids remain always material or corporal. You write as much in your book: "Thus, in our time, any attempt to interrupt the slow movement of architecture, to artificially adapt it to the acceleration of the rhythm of space by the introduction of notions of high speed like evolution, technology, mobility, flexibility, are doomed to failure..."

I still believe it's true. Speed is carrying us along, but we have yet to master it. An accident is bound to happen, so when I talk about dromology or dromocracy I mean inventing a political economy of speed just as we innovated a political economy of wealth. The two are connected in my thinking. I am certain that as long as we do not bring about the dromocratic or dromological revolution, we are heading for the total, the global accident. And certainly one way of reducing speed is the dwelling. The very word in French for building, "im-meuble," un-moving, and the word for dwelling, "demeure," to stay or remain—they are the speed reducers of history. No one can deny that the city reduced the speed of the nomads by sedentariness. We are faced with the necessity of reinventing a politics of speed, whose means and place should be the city, since the city [*polis*] and politics are connected.

Slowness can be a means of resistance. Inclined planes slow down movement.

In my view, slowness is just one speed among many, don't you agree? I never talk about slowness.

I am talking about slowness as intensity. The gait of nomads in the desert is always extremely slow and aquatic. In the Sahara people move like kings or scuba divers, it's extraordinary. And it's not just due to the heat: in Timbuctu a Touareg friend of mine told me that as a child he was asked to walk even slower. Each of their gestures in slow motion had an unimaginable grace. For them walking was a dance. And yet they jumped on top of their camels like tigers.

That's why I'm interested in William Forsythe, in choreography.[24] Speed is choreography. Sometimes it goes really fast, sometimes really slow. The body movements of time and space is what I call choreography.

It's the Sumo wrestler frozen like a statue and then...

...and then wham! The tiger. That's politics. There is a politics of bodies in dance that was forgotten in the industrial revolution, all in favor of the robot, in favor of the car in which you are tossed around.

Like the oblique, the body collapses space into time.

Oh yes. From the moment you consider a human body in motion—this is the choreographic dimension, and not simply the geographic and scenographic dimensions: the gesture of the body in space—the question of time is raised. Dance is an art of time, just like the theater.

The Two Spaces

Even in the architecture of the future?

Yes. Except that now there are two spaces. I am speaking here only of architecture and dance—let's be clear on that. At one time there was only actual space, the space of the act, and of course the virtualization of dream, of painting, of music, etc. Whereas today, next to actual space there is now virtual space, the space of action through tele-action, tele-sexuality, tele-surgery from a distance, tele-olfaction, tele-feel, tele-touch, tele-sight. It's only tele-taste that doesn't work yet. All the senses are carried at a distance. The result is that next to actual space, which has been the space of history, there is now virtual space, and the two are interdependent. We have before us a stereo reality. Like the lows and the highs that create a field effect, a relief effect, we now have actual space and virtual space. And the architect has to work with both. Just as the architects of Versailles worked with the Hall of Mirrors. Except that now it is not simply a phenomenon of representation; it is a place of action. The presence of an avatar is a semi-real presence. But through an avatar you can kill from a distance; you need only look at the techniques of infowar. Thus you have to work with this stereo reality, with this relief of reality. We are heading toward a world in which the Quattrocento's perspective of space is no longer sufficient. We need an Alberti, a Brunelleschi ...

Or a Paolo Uccello: he was a mad explorer of lost dimensions ...

... to create a real-time perspective for virtual space. And you have to deal with both. That is the world of tomorrow. It's the world of the tele-city, of the meta-city, the world of tele-politics and tele-war. It's the world of tele-sexuality. We have before us a virtual space that is a space of procreation, and not simply a space of pleasure. So what does this mean? It means that tele-portation is already here, cloning is already here. I feel like saying: today tele-action is already cloning. Tele-action is being at a distance. It is being doubled. Before, being was the *hic et nunc*, the body was the *hic et nunc* ...

Now the body no longer has any shadow.

There is no longer a shadow. Thus there are certain things at work here which affect architecture, politics, etc. But I'm quitting architecture. Moreover, I'd like to say that this dialogue will be my last. Why? Because the whole thing is starting over in France. I'll explain. In the sixties, when I was working on the "oblique function" with Claude Parent, no one took me seriously. OK. And I wound up in teaching. A year ago I left behind the teaching of architecture to work on these two spaces, on this cybernetic space which connects at once actual space and virtual space. But even old friends don't seem to understand that. They say: Virilio is acting up again.

And you are the first to know: I am retiring from architecture. I don't want to hear any more about it. The city, yes, let's keep talking about it. But architecture, it's finished, over. Curtain.

You're still interested in housing, though.

Well, that's true. French architects have built monuments and facilities, but the place where you reform and revolutionize architecture is the house. The last assignment I had my students at the École Spéciale do was "Exit House." You spend Sunday in a convivial room, then transit via the bedroom or the bathroom and wake up in Monday's room. You move every day and everyday of the week corresponds to a specific setting. It's a topological house, a way of raising the question of time in space and this brings about a change in the very structure of the house.

The house and the city—the two poles of your work.

The city, because today politics is urban; the city is world. We are already in the *world city*. There are local cities and "global cities." The local cities are the subdivisions of a world city linked together by virtual space, by the markets, tele-action, webcams, etc. We have carried through the remark Namatianus made to Caesar: "You have made the world a city." Through super-rapid, super-fast means of transportation, and through cybernetic means of telecommunication, we are de facto in an urban world system—even if, of course, huge regions remain untouched, Africa and elsewhere. Something political is being played out here which concerns the urban planner and, I would say, the citizen. Now that interests me. Why? Because we are in a populating period. Once again in the history of mankind we have great migratory movements, not circumstantial but structural, and we are entering one of these great periods. If you look at the recent history of Europe—Europe is the continent of sedentariness, contrary to Africa, contrary to Asia, contrary even to America—you realize that the nineteenth century opposes the city to the country; the twentieth century opposes the city to the suburb (we're still there); and the twenty-first century opposes the resident to the nomad. But watch out: residents now are not those who are stuck at home, but those who are everywhere at home thanks to their cell phones. They're "wired." That's Steve Mann.

This reminds me of what you said of the Palestinian people in Popular Defense and Ecological Struggles.[25] *Uprooted from their soil, Palestinians experienced a "national delocalization," extending their political boundaries to the runways of international airports, and from there to the entire world by colonizing the airwaves. At the time, in the late seventies, you saw their tragedy as the way of the future. Now it's become the way privileged residents themselves live: they are able to transcend national localizations and be at home anywhere through telecommunication.*

The residents are at home everywhere, on the train, in a jet while the nomads are at home nowhere: homeless, migrants who only have a jalopy to live in. If they take up a collection, they can put some gas in and go elsewhere. Or they have huts made out of cardboard in the subway. There you have the future. Social mobility becomes a phenomenon that is no longer circumstantial and linked to unemployment, but linked to the crisis of work as a place of sedentarization through contracts of indeterminate length and through a binding of the workforce within proximity of employment pockets. We are entering the new nomadic era. I have no doubt that this is a world-populating phenomenon, and not simply an immigration problem from South to North or from East to West. This is a phenomenon of mutation like the one we had ten centuries ago, or at the beginning of the population of the world. And we are only at the very beginning.

Polar Inertia

Today a resident simply is a traveling owner.

But in reality it's polar inertia. These people don't move, even when they're in a high-speed train. They don't move when they travel in their jet. They are residents in absolute motion— -speed, the super-speed of the train, or the supersonic jet, or the super-fast boat, and the super-speed of instantaneous telecommunication which allows them to play the stock market instantaneously on Wall Street or in Hong Kong.

And the nomads are the dispossessed.

The nomads are the poor. We are moving towards a category of people who are nowhere at home.

They are the ones you wrote about in Chambres précaires [Precarious Rooms], *the poignant photo-album by Jacqueline Salmon,*[26] *which documents imprints of these displacements, traces of an uninhabitable circulation, "waiting rooms without platforms…"*

The famous deregulation of international transport isn't just the cheap tickets for pleasure trip of mass tourism, it is also stowaways, runaway children, boat people, illegal immigrants coming from everywhere. And I choose to side with them. With Father Giros, we just opened a shelter near the Gare du Nord.

We go back to Marx's theory of absolute pauperization, with the difference that it is no longer about the working class, but about those without class and without a place… Now it is the workers themselves who have become the owners.

Yes, it is the end of mankind as a work force in favor of the machine. What Marx did not foresee is that when one no longer needs people, they are not masters for all that. They are nothing. The end of mankind as producer, the end of mankind as progenitor (we're headed towards engineering, test-tube babies, sperm donors), the end of mankind as destroyers (you don't need soldiers anymore: drones, cruise missiles, you send them off the way you send dogs)—it's the end of humanity. We are faced with an apocalyptic time. This explains the clones, the idea of eugenics to create high performance men and women.

They will no longer be owners, but owned...

And then the Supermen are like trans-genetic produce: they will be resistant to everything. There will be the genetically correct and the genetically incorrect. You and I are uteros, born from the filth of sperm and the secretions of a vagina, how disgusting. We are dirty.

A return to fascism...

Whereas the others...

...they're pure.

They're clean. That's the new eugenics. But anything can happen. All the same, it is exciting.

So how do you raise the question of architecture today in this era of globalization?

There is an architecture of globalization just like there was an internationalist architecture, an architecture inspired for the most part by Mies van der Rohe and by the formal purists who came from Bauhaus, having left Germany for obvious reasons. The most important pole for the architecture of globalization is *temporal compression*. Contrary to the fifties and sixties when everyone was mostly talking about space, now you have to talk about time. Temporal compression is a technical term. It illustrates that real time is a determining element of power. Temporal compression is what I also call "dromospheric pressure" in reference to atmospheric pressure.

Standardization/Synchronization

Isn't that paradoxical, putting time first when talking about architecture?

Yes. Moreover, people haven't quite followed because they haven't made it yet to space-time and that's the big problem. In the twentieth century, a modular standardization in the space of production was secured by the post-war recontruction through prefabrication; after which the twenty-first century's synchronization of the time of communication became imperative. *Standardization* and *synchronization* are the two sides of modern architecture's space-time.

World time has come to dominate local time.

The world time of history, of chronicles, almanacs, and calendars has been overcome, dominated, by the world time of "real time," in other words, the time of instantaneousness, ubiquity, immediacy. Hence free trade. Hence the necessity of leaping over borders, but over agreements as well, and of arriving at an unfettered, permanent flow, favorable to synchronization. In my view, you can't understand anything about the WTO, the World Trade Organization, and the frantic will to free up trade, without understanding the will—after the standardization of the industrial period—to enter into the reign of synchronization in the post-industrial period.

We haven't yet left behind standardization, for all that.

No, the two are coupled together. The other important pole for an architect today is the relation to the body. But it's a relation that goes beyond traditional ergonomics. It is not a question of the Vitruvian man or of the proportions you find in certain books like the Neufert [a German book of architectural standards], where you have every ergonomic proportion to situate the work space perfectly, etc. It's about the ergonomics of the space-time of being, an ergonomics which does not exist, but which is to be put together from the dynamics of being, through what I have called the "energetic being," no longer an ergonomic being. These two aspects, then, obviously raise a host of questions. In the globalization period, everything is being played out between two themes, or two terms: *foreclosure*[27] and "exclusion," which you call in English the *locked-in syndrom*. It's the syndrome of confinement.

It's confinement under an open sky.

Exactly. The locked-in syndrom is a rare neurological state that translates as complete paralysis, an inability to speak, but with one's consciousness and intellectual faculties perfectly intact. The setting up of synchronization and free trade is the temporal compression of interactivity. The temporal compression of interactivity reacts on the real space of our usual immediate activities. You can't understand globalization without thinking about *activity* as well as *mentality*. I use the term "mentality" in the old sense of the word. Let's not forget that if the world proper of the philosopher is outside of ourselves, it is equally inside of the body proper. This is what the English call "cognitive mapping," those mental images which are vital for the orientation of our action. The world is inside of us. I have a figure of the world within me. I have a figure of Paris, my neighborhood, my house, within me. And it all interacts together.

Temporal Compression

Your dwelling is a habitat in the architectural sense. The architecture of the world is a mental construct.

Your dwelling is your habitat in the ecological sense, and your house in an architectural sense. Thus *temporal compression*, i.e. the escalation to the maximum speed of interactivity, modifies the cognitive map. Every time you have an orientation in space, you have a relation of space and time. Does it take me six months to go to China, or six hours? Will it take me two seconds, or two hours? Thus temporal compression acts on the body proper through the intermediary of the world proper which has been modified in the consciousness of the individual. Here we enter into the ergonomics of the individual's time proper, that is, the representation that the individual creates for himself of his environment from the largest to the smallest scale.

So the larger the space is, the more it contracts within me.

The space-time of the local distances in which "I" live is inscribed in an apprehension of the global distances which surround me. At this moment Paris is within me. I don't need maps or landmarks. It is enough for me to start walking to orient myself. But this is true of the Ile de France that surrounds Paris, as well as of France in its entirety. I have France within me. Why? Because I have already traversed it, because I have already internalized it, because the mental figuration, the mental mapping, has been made of my travels, my experiences. The same goes for Europe. The world proper is composed within me of the speeds of transference and transmission that have constructed me—my body proper inside the world proper. This situation of interference between local distances and global distances, which is modified by speed, explains the present contraction. It is in the end a contraction in the sense of a compression between the exterior and the interior of the body proper. The body proper no longer has the same relationship to the world proper as it did during the Crusades or in the days of Marco Polo.

The body proper is contracted ...

And the world proper is contracting ... The contraction of distances in travel leads to the contraction of the world proper, but through a phenomenon of resonance, an echo effect, the body proper itself takes on a considerable importance.

The body proper is being contracted through speed, the disappearance of space in time.

The world is getting too small. And since the world proper is getting too small, the body proper takes on more importance, which explains individualism. You know what I'm saying. Societies of collectivism were societies in which there were still significant temporal distances. Hence the possibility, moreover, of long-distance war: recall the forty thousand tanks of the Soviet Union. When you see how today everything is played out in an instant, well, this contraction of the space-time of political or military action is also a contraction of the day-to-day life of individuals. Hence the present contraction between the exterior and the interior of the body proper is called *glocalization*, which is added to the traditional term, "globalization." Faced with this situation, I don't think we can forget the term "glocalization."

The local is the glocal.

On the one hand you have the global of the local, and on the other you have simply the global. Thus you have a fractal dimension taking hold. In effect, multimedia interactivity is nothing but the echo effect, the resonance, of world enclosure. In other words, when you speak in an echo chamber, your words come back immediately. That's all interactivity is! Interactivity would not be possible if the distances of the world equaled those of the galaxy. Interactivity is possible because the earth is small, and the speed of light makes it so that in a few fractions of a second I can interact, inter-see, inter-hear, etc.

Instantaneous feedback.

In fact, media interactivity is nothing but the echo effect, the echo chamber, of the closure of the world, this terrestrial globe which has become too small for the media activity of mankind. Interactivity results from the pressure of instantaneous real time on the real space of succession. You see, we have on the one hand the pressure of real time and on the other simultaneity. Interactivity is the catching up of simultaneity with the real space of chronological and historical succession.

Interactivity is not the kind of dialogue or exchange that it is often assumed to be. Quite the contrary ...

No sooner said than done. Wow.

No more dialogue, no more stage. We're no longer communicating. Communication itself is communicated without leaving a trace.

It proves that we are now in a closed box. We're in a closed world. What people take to be the payoff of interactivity is only the sign of enclosure. It is thus impossible to talk here about urbanism and globalization without evoking foreclosure, in other words, the incarceration of which we are already the unconscious victims. For a long time now, I have had the feeling that we are heading toward an unbearable way of life. I'll explain. The body proper of our habitat has become not only unhealthy due to the pollution of the substances that make it up—this is green ecology—but soon uninhabitable, or almost, due to the sudden pollution of temporal distances, these intervals that threaten the world's geophysics. The world of green ecology is unhealthy, and the world of *grey* ecology is becoming uninhabitable. Because it's too small. And because after a while, this interactivity becomes unbearable.

Grey Ecology

Grey ecology would be the ecology of distances.

In my view, to the pollution of nature, of substances, has been added the pollution of distances, that is, the pollution of the real-life proportion. In what we call nature, there are not only substances, but distances too. This is the architect speaking: the proportions which surround us are part and parcel of ecology. Dimensions count. A man twenty feet tall would be in a different relation to the world and to others. This situation, the retention of the distances of the world proper, is what I would call an incarceration effect, a confinement effect, which is much more serious than the one that Foucault denounced in the disciplinary society of the eighteenth century. The confinement that I am announcing is on a whole other level having nothing to do with a penitentiary attitude.

The body used to be confined in space, and now it is time that imprisons us.

It is the body in time, in a space-time too infinitely compressed for man not to feel a fundamental claustrophobia.

Polar inertia is no longer a movement toward extremes, but is at the very foundation of interactivity.

It's the tendency that leads to polar inertia. We've heard a lot about the greenhouse effect in the atmosphere, carbon gases and the ozone, but that still accounts for only the one side of the pollution of nature: substance. Now there exists a second pollution, invisible but not imperceptible, contaminating the real-life geospheric proportions of the planet. This second greenhouse effect is *dromospheric*, resulting from the pressure of hyper- and supersonic transportation speeds, transportation of goods and people, but mostly from the speed of cybernetic transmission of action at a distance, not to mention "escape velocity," which lets you blast off. The critical space of which I spoke, when William Gibson was talking about virtual space and cyberspace, this critical space is thus in fact another name for virtual space and, as they say, its "augmented reality," whereas in my view the correct term would be "accelerated reality." Again, virtual reality is an effect of acceleration, of calculation. The acceleration of transmission is not an invention that has just come about. It is the result of the great race that began with the taming of horses, the invention of ships, motors, etc.

Critical Space

Your term "critical" should be understood in the sense of "crisis."

Yes, in the sense of space being put into a state of crisis. A critical time—you know that it's a time that will pass. The man who is going to die in five seconds is in critical temporality; he's reached the end. But in this case, it is the real space of the globe—not space in the sense of outer space, cosmic space—that is critical. As I said in my book, *Lost Dimension*, it was no longer just time that was critical, the critical moment; the new thing was that space itself had entered a critical dimension with relativity and at the same time with the fractals. On the one hand, you have relativity, space-time, philosophy: Bergson, Einstein. On the other hand, you have whole dimensions called into question, which is an important event that went unnoticed. We imploded dimensions. History has lived through whole dimensions: zero dimension, the point, line and surface; here you find Kandinsky, volume plus time. One dimension, two dimensions, three dimensions. This is fundamental in the West: the history of the relationship in space with Greece, with the perspectivists, etc. Then we exploded it. So, I wanted to say that the big event was critical space.Critical space is at the intersection of relativity, the fractals, and of course the notion of the accident, since the Big Bang is the origin of history and what gives us dimensions. But now we explode them. Whole dimensions are simulacra. So you have this fundamental anxiety linked to the notion of space. You cannot separate the notion of space from the notion of dimension. In the East, it is well known that the notion of dimension doesn't exist, but it is replaced by the *Ma*, the interval. It is the equivalent of the interval in music.

This is really important. In the East, the musical interval in the tempo also has to do with the interval in space. Dimensions don't exist without going through the interval. And here I will refer you to the "Third Interval," one of the chapters in *Speed and Politics*.

If it is the crisis of earth space, architecture, being the art of that space, should be in crisis as well.

Critical space is the dimension of the retention of distances: this pollution of temporal distances through interactivity is already leading to effects of claustrophobia and incarceration, which are going to be the big questions for urbanism and architecture tomorrow. Faced with this sudden foreclosure of the real space of globalization, resulting from the temporal compression of inter-activity, exclusion becomes a necessity with the "global-city," implying a new relationship to bodies, to the territorial bodies of the geographic habitat.

Exclusion with respect to what exactly?

With respect to critical space. The body proper is not outside a world proper, a world that has been appropriated. The world proper was the world of the terrestrial globe. All of history, the whole of psychology, all of philosophy happened within a sym-biosis of these two elements: world proper, body proper. The absolute retention of the body proper leads the individual to be excluded from this world. Hence all the research to leave the goddamn planet behind. Many of the practices since the Second World War, including the conquest of space by the Nazis, already are attempts to achieve exclusion. To exclude oneself from a world that is too small.

It's the lebensraum—*the breathing space—and the right to expand territorially in the Nazis' case.*

Exactly, the right to exclude oneself from an incarcerating world. Exclusion becomes a psychological necessity that implies a new relation to bodies, to the terrestrial bodies of the geographic habitat, but also to the social body of geopolitical societies, and finally to the animal body of an individual caught in mass individualism. Ancient societies were different in that they were collective masses, and the world itself used to be vast. We're back to the same effect I mentioned earlier. Faced with the compression of the world proper, individualism becomes dominant. This is the fractal aspect of being. The body becomes the whole. Hence mass egoism, mass egotism, mass individualism. We still live in a mass society, yes! but *a mass society of individuals.* In this way, after centuries, millennia dedicated to the urbanization of the real space of the world proper—it's the history of cities since the dawn of time—now begins the urbanization of the real time of the body proper of mankind. Hence synchronization. The cybernetic synchronization of collective interactivity is replacing the old standardization of activity—the standardized social behaviors and disciplinary behaviors from the age of mass collectivism.

Portable-Self

So forget Foucault?

No more Foucault either. On that topic, Professor Kevin Warwick's recent experiment considered to be a lark, in which he implanted in his own body an electric chip to interact with his working environment, is the beginning of a new way of life. I said it a number of years ago: the transplant revolution is nothing but the colonization of the body by technology. You have again the contraction between the world proper equipped with Roman ways, railways, highways, and the body proper equipped with bionics and microchips, etc. After the era of home-city domestic life during the fifties and sixties, thanks to the electric cleaner, the TV, comes not only the era of the portable city "on-self," such as the computer and the cell phone, but now the era of the "in-self," when implants, bionic prostheses, and other electrodes wire us up. The movement is always the same: simply, instead of saddling the body of the world with equipment, you equip the body of the individual.

It's also another form of nomadism, but internal, so to speak. The body has become the world.

The world proper is no longer only outside; it is inside.

The habitat is the inhabitant.

The inhabitant becomes the habitat...of technology. He is "phagocyted," if you prefer. And that's what *exclusion* is, you see. A man who is equipped like a territory is no longer an inhabitant; he becomes a habitat.

He is no longer only mentally inhabited, but physically too. He is no longer habited; he is in-habited.

Architecture possesses him. Now I remind you that in computer talk they refer to the "system architecture." The word "architecture" doesn't just qualify buildings of brick or concrete, it refers to a system. There is not only a system architecture, but one of habits. Warwick is in instantaneous interaction through his body, no longer through his will, but through the grafts, electrodes, and microchips that occupy him.

The Architecture of Feedback

And this is a kind of prefiguration of the architecture to come...

Yes. Architecture today is an *exorbitant habitat*. The habit becomes the habitat. The robe-tent of Greek or Turk shepherds, or the equipment of the scuba diver, were the first forms of this habit-habitat before the modification of organs by implants, etc. You have examples already of this with underwater divers whose respiratory organs are modified so they can be more at ease under water. Temporal or dromospheric compression—they're the same—and the untimely appearance of an interactivity in the process of global generalization are soon going to raise a question that is eccentric *par excellence*: the architecture of feedback. In other words, the question of retro-control and retro-action. The architecture of feedback is no longer concerned only with man and machine, as in the period of early cybernetics—we know that feedback is the man-machine interface of Norbert Wiener— but now between the body and the human milieu, between the body proper and the world proper, whose retention has become unbearable on account of its closeness. A spatio-temporal milieu that is foreclosed, where the importance of ubiquity, but mostly of simultaneity, is winning out over the space-time of historic and chronological succession. And this is crucial. In the era of simultaneity, succession loses its importance. This isn't Francis Fukuyama's end of history, but it is the end of chronology, that is, of the transition: past, present, future.

In architectural terms, this would mean that buildings will no longer be conceived as the succession of spaces, but in terms of temporal compression. Simultaneity is still compression. The present dominates.

Absolutely. Rooms, passageways, hallways, etc. We are moving toward a feedback, i.e., toward a telescoping, of architectures that will have to react with the instantaneity of communication. Elements of this are already in place: virtual portals. We know that thanks to the data suit, the information suit, they have already envisioned the existence of a portal, a place where a man can enter by means of his *specter*—not by means of his avatar as with the ordinary computer today, but his specter. I'll take an example: you have a friend in New York, and you want to meet up with him or her at all costs. Well, you go into your room in Paris, and they go into theirs in New York: a virtual portal, like a telephone booth. Before going in, you equip yourself with a data suit, with data gloves, you don your visio-helmet, you go in, you shake the hand of his specter (or you kiss the specter of your wife), you speak to them, you can even feel their body. Thus your friend's presence is a spectral presence, present only on account of the speed of sensory transmissions, on account of the feedback pressure on the gloves and body, and also on account of the television or tele-audition or tele-olfaction.

It's the total expansion of the telephone, as Mallarmé was dreaming of the total expansion of the letter. A tele-world.

In a way, it is the beginning of teleportation. But only in a way, because the vision we have of teleportation in comic strips or science fiction has the body decompose particle by particle to be recomposed afterward. It is a substantialist vision and not, as I would say, a distancialist vision. The virtual portal is teleportation, but the teleportation of the specter of proportions. And of the specter of communication. There would be much to say on the question of the specter and the question of the image. Here we touch on the religious dimension. How do you raise the question of the body or the object with respect to the image, on the first level, without raising the question of the body with respect to the specter? We know that the specter was taken seriously in every ancient society. Not in the sense of ghosts, but as the result of the presence of spirits, so to speak. The presence of spirits was taken seriously, as was the image. But today we have put the image on a pedestal—civilization of the image, virtual reality, etc. We forget that with the information suit, the data suit, with all that I have just described, well, you have a return of the specter.

Tele-Presence

And the beginnings of a spectral architecture—in any case its end as a purely spatial project.

What I am saying above is that the question of ergonomics must raise this particular problem, the problem of the presence of the body at a distance. Tele-presence. For four years I gave a course at the International College of Philosophy in Paris on tele-presence, and everybody was there except the philosophers. But this is the philosophical question par excellence. What is tele-presence with respect to presence? What is teleportation with respect to presentation? These are the big questions. Were there an Aristotle, a Plato, not to mention a Heidegger, they would be on top of it, they would have already written three treatises on it ...

A=Non-A. It's the end of the logic of identity, the law of the nonexcluded middle. Something like an induced telephrenia or technophrenia.

At this stage, the mutation of urbanization, but also of architecture, will probably compel the development of a topological logic. Orthogonal, Euclidian forms had to do with succession, but as soon as you introduce simultaneity, it requires the development of a topological logic for the architect. The control of gravity by static and the resistance of materials—but also the control of natural light by optics—will necessarily be added to the control of interactivity, of feedback, by computer science and tele-science. Now the third necessity of architectonics, and thus of construction, will result from harnessing the body proper of the inhabitant in the third millennium.

Time has become dominant, but space hasn't disappeared for that matter.

Except that it is in crisis, and speed is no longer the speed of life, the speed of a horse, or even the speed of the wind. But you can say that we have acquired superior speeds, including the escape velocity which liberates us from gravity. And it is with this speed that we are going to build the relation of interactivity with the architectural and urban milieu. In a foreclosed, shut-out world, within confinement, a geographic confinement.

A return to the bunker-monad "without walls or windows ..."

The one who is saying all this is the same who worked on the bunkers forty years ago. I feel like saying that the world, the planet, is becoming a blockhouse, a closed house, foreclosed.

And it is from within this foreclosure, and not from within a world made smaller by globalization, that we can begin to envision the new architecture. It is not on the inside—the illusion of the great scale of globalization. Globalization is the world becoming too small, and not too big. Thus it is from within this claustrophobic consciousness, a consciousness of incarceration and massive confinement, not the disciplinary confinement of Foucault, but of technology, that the question of urbanization and of architecture is to be raised. So we're outside everything that is being debated right now.

Architecture will project itself here into the time of interactivity, or into outer space ...

I don't want to make science-fiction of architecture: I've done some, and I don't want to go back to that. What I mean is that tomorrow's city is being constructed with the idea of leaving the planet behind. The planet is becoming uninhabitable. When I say that, I'm thinking in term of the era of the millenary. But it's unstoppable. We are not going to go back to speeds from five centuries ago. We have closed the door behind us thanks to the rapidity of interactivity, and we will build from within the perspective of an earth that is too small. Not only too small because of overpopulation, but because we have reduced the world to nothing. So it's from within this claustrophobic consciousness that urban architecture, indeed any and all architecture, can be constructed. And they will be constructed on the new body, an autonomous body, a body that is no longer the body of individualism, but the self-sufficient body of the spacewalker. The spacewalker is the image of man-as-planet. When you watch astronaut Scott Carpenter walk above the earth in his little spatial scooter, he is man-as-planet, a satellite. And such a man, I'm not sure that he represents progress as compared to us. He reminds me more of a life raft.

Escape from Humanity

Architecture is no longer in an earthly dwelling, but in an escape vehicle that sticks to the body like a space suit, the clothing that you carry with you. Could you briefly recapitulate in conclusion how we have arrived to this situation?

Every word counts here: synchronization is bringing standardization to completion. Interactivity is just the evidence of foreclusion. Hence the possibility of an extra-world, an out-world habitat. Here you must indeed ask yourself: how did we get to this point? The world is foreclosed because we have implemented the absolute speed of waves which permits interactivity, and supersonic and hypersonic speed in the transportion of bodies. That's what foreclusion is. We have made the world too small, foreclosed. As for the exclusion, it is obvious that the acquisition of escape velocity will allow us to liberate ourselves from the habitat, to exclude ourselves from the world, and thus to become autonomous, to become a planet-man like Carpenter. It is a problem of speed, not temporality or space. Speed makes history…

By unmaking it…

Yes, but the other aspect is clearly the possibility of work on the body itself, on the animal body itself, thanks to the speed of the computer which is the equivalent of escape velocity for the body proper. Speed facilitates the decoding of the human genome and the possibility of an other humanity, a humanity which is no longer the one we know. It is now no longer a question of the extra-terrestrial, but of the extra-human.

II

THE GENETIC BOMB

1. EUGENICS

Two Intrusive Offensives □ Three Revolutions in Speed □ Cyborg □ Endo-Colonization □ Three Bodies □ Artificial Selection □ Genetic Robots □ Super-Racism □ Auschwitz-Birkenau □ Mass Killers □ Human Experiments □ Teratology □ Art of the Camps □ Body-Art □ Extreme Sciences □ Abjection □ Transgenic Art □ Reinventing Myths □ Anesthesia, Euthanasia □ Apathy □ Cruelty

Two Offensives

We said that the body is becoming everything but at the same time it is being penetrated by technology in every possible way. Even the labeling of genes is a superlative form of invasion.

Yes, but we mustn't confuse them. In my opinion, there are two intrusive offensives, what I would call two points of attack on the body. And I don't think we ought to mix them up. On the one hand, we have what is called *bionics*, which I prefer to call *flesh-eating prosthetics* [phagocitage des prothèses]. This is the first point of attack: technological prostheses that interface with the body. I will come back to that. And on the other hand, we have *information technology*, in other words, the decoding of DNA, the mapping of the human genome, the opening of the "book of life." So these are the two offensives.

There is nevertheless a relation between the two: in a sense with the human genome it is the entire body that is becoming a prosthetics of technology.

Three Revolutions

You may say so, but it is still two quite different phases. Bionics is the first phase, which I have called the "third revolution" in speed. If you like, I can go back over it a little. Three revolutions in speed divide three centuries, from the nineteenth to the twenty-first. The first, from the nineteenth century well into the twentieth century, is the revolution in *transportation*. Its heroes could be Jules Verne and Howard Hughes, each in his own way. The second is the revolution in *transmissions*, whose hero could be Steve Mann or Jaron Lanier. And the revolution in *transplants*, of course, is the third: that's Professor Warwick. Warwick, an Englishman, had a microship sewn into himself to avoid wearing a badge while walking around his laboratory and his university. Everybody laughed at him. But in a society where security is no longer guaranteed, where information is central and the loss of information is a national drama, it is obvious that carrying cards around is a weak spot. Furthemore, it's a real pain to spend your time entering codes when you're moving in a highly policed space. Thanks to the chip integrated within it, Warwick's body enters the codes in a state of relaxation. So, you see, we have three characters and three revolutions.

*Let's look at these characters first. Like Hegel, you often try to con-
dense the various contradictions and innovations of a period in a
single hero, the way you often bounce an idea with a striking quote.
But for you they are more than representatives of their times, they
embody an idea poetically through their own excess.*

Many people don't understand how passionate I am about these
personalities that go to the limit. It's the same with Artaud, Kafka,
Hannah Arendt, Simone Weil. I have always felt the same way.

*Probably because you always try to go to the limit yourself. The first
hero you brought out in* Pure War *was Howard Hughes. Hughes was
an exemplary figure of the revolution in transportation. He foreshadowed a mass situation because even though he owned the world
of speed (movie studios, planes, etc.), he ended up a total recluse. He
became our first "technological monk," a man who experienced to the
extreme the reversion of speed into polar inertia.[28] Steve Mann, the
hero of the revolution in transmissions, is a fascinating character too,
and it would be worth following up his itinerary as well in some
details. A professor of engineering from Toronto, for the last thirty
years he's been wearing a headset ("eyetap glasses") as if it were a part
of his own body. His glasses actually act as a very compact electronic
studio since they contain several lasers, diminutive video-cameras
and half-a dozen tiny computers strapped on his body in a fanny
pack. This vision system allows him to record, interpret and "aug-
ment" his everyday experiences. I assumed at first that Steve Mann
acted as he did out of his love for technology, but I was mistaken. On
the contrary, his intention is to fight the invasion of "totalitarian
technology" in everyday life the way Louis Wolfson, the famous
"shizophrenic student of languages," resisted his mother tongue by
wearing a walkman at all times. Far from being a "tech-head," Steve*

Mann is a self-styled techno-vigilante, a more benign forerunner of the Unabomber. While Howard Hughes was undone by his own technological achievements, Mann managed to move everywhere protected by his own electronic bubble. He insisted, though, on "shooting back" at surveillance cameras by recording everything he saw or by projecting his own messages directly on his retina to protect himself from public advertisement. Needless to say, this guerilla software didn't especially endear him to the various controlling agencies, from police stations to chain-stores and casinos which he openly challenged with his own equipment. And yet his exclusive reliance on sophisticated technology also exposed the glaring weaknesses of his subversive enterprise. Returning to Toronto in the aftermath of September 11, he met with a much stiffer resistance from airport security personnel who brutally unplugged him from his technology, stripped-searched and injured him (they tore the electrodes from his skin) causing serious damage to his half-a-million dollars wearable computers. Suddenly the "wired Mann" found himself disoriented and incapable of performing the simplest task. After a three-day ordeal, he bumped against a pile of fire extinguishers and passed out. Finally he had to board the plane in a wheelchair, a casualty of the revolution in transmission which he tried to oppose through similar means.[29]

Mann anticipated Warwick, that is, the intrusion of technology in the body.

Now Warwick has a new implant capable of sending signals back and forth between his nervous system and a computer, altering the way he senses reality. Jaron Lanier did it another way. I know that he is a computer scientist best known for his work on Virtual Reality and that his vision is very optimistic. He is convinced that technology will be leading humanity to some kind of utopian interactive future. What makes him another hero of the revolution in transmissions?

With a few other people, he is the hero of the data-suit, which allows someone to interact at a distance with a body, or transfer oneself into another body. So, these are the three characters for the three revolutions. The revolution in *physical transportation* came first: movement and acceleration up to supersonic speeds. The revolution in *transmissions*, which comes second, is the revolution of live transmission. It is the cybernetic revolution. It is the ability to reach the light barrier, in other words, the speed of electromagnetic waves in every field, not only television and tele-audition, but also tele-operation. Finally, the revolution in *transplants*, the last revolution, introduces this technology of transmission inside the body by means of certain techniques. After the revolution in transportation and the revolution in transmissions, now with the twenty-first century begins the revolution in intra-organic transplants.

The revolution in transmissions is the one that offers the possibility of decoding the information contained in the human genome.

Yes, the information program of the living organism. And there you have what I just said a minute ago about the "book of life," the decoding of the DNA. So, let's first take the revolution in transplants. The revolution in transplants illustrates the will of the Futurists to feed the body no longer on proteins, that is, on the sort of cannibalism which is characteristic of humans— humans are carnivorous, they devour plants and animals—but to have it feed itself on technology and energy by means of implants—from the pacemaker, which was the first fundamental transplant, on up to additional memory, microchips, bionics, incorporated telephones, etc. I won't go into the details here, but we should re-read Marinetti, in any case we shouldn't forget what he says about bodies, because this desire goes back to the Futurists, and thus to fascism. Marinetti is a prophet of fascism. Not only the fascism of Mussolini, but also the eugenic fascism of Josef Mengele. And he foresaw it. This is the phase that I have called flesh-eating prosthetics.

Technology may provoke these revolutions, but art is capable of anticipating them.

Art is initiatory. Certainly since Romanticism, since the eighteenth and the nineteenth centuries in any case, the arts have been, in the profane sense of the word, prophetic of political mutations. One can say that in some way the arts had a role comparable to religion and philosophy. But the role of art was not to question the world, the way philosophy and religion did; the role of art was to announce prophetically what was in the offing.

Endo-Colonization of the Body

Talking about prophecy, twenty years ago, in Pure War, *we envisaged the "endo-colonization" of South America by their own military not as a symptom of underdevelopment but, on the contrary, as a laboratory for societies to come. The occupation of one's own population was foreshadowing a situation that was eventually extended to the rest of the world with the enforcement of a "minimal state" and the abandonment of entire populations, starting with the homeless. And this phenomenon has taken on even more catastrophic proportions with the advent of globalization. The colonization of the body by biotechnology is very much part of the same phenomenon. It could be said that the artificial insertion of micro-machines into the body is extending the type of territorial colonization that Europe has imposed over the world, inside.*

The colonial utopia *par excellence* is the attempt to modify the body of the colonized. When I say that, I am not referring to the state of the colonized, but to a state of fact, to techno-science, to the state of the world. A colonial, imperial, total power has never been exercised over a country without simultaneously exercising this colonial, imperial or total power over the body. This power can be found in drilling. Then you come to realize that biotechnologies are, on the scale of the world empire, the same as the drill to the army, or the training of bodies meant to civilize "savages" in colonies. Except that in the present situation the problem is not to civilize savage bodies, but to modify living bodies through cloning, through chimeras.

Biotechnology is a way of preparing bodies for a global world as the internet was a way of preparing the entire population for electronic warfare. The biological revolution basically extends the reach of globalization by opening a free market inside. Already, from China to Romania, there's a thriving black-market extorting spare parts from third word bodies to benefit first-world countries.

It's a new form of training which, like totalitarian utopias, aims at creating a new type of human being. But here the new individual is not simply the Aryan, or Foucault's discipline subject, but the new human of biology. A human being no longer procreated, born out of another, but *created*. It is the end of the *sui generis*.

Three Bodies

The new human of biology corresponds to the cloning of the world itself through the transmission technologies.

We don't have a body outside the world. We have a *territorial* body, a *social* body (or socius*)*, and an *animal* body. The first body is the world. Without the world proper, the social body and the body proper don't exist. Technology colonized external space first by means of the Roman roads, of the great canals, of high-voltage wires, infra-structures, and it is now colonizing the animal body. The territorial body is more important than the socius or the animal body. If there is no land, there are no humans. The first mortality occurs when the relation between the body proper and the world is cut off. There is no example of anything alive, of any live body without a world. The territorial loss, in this respect, cannot be compared to the one that results from the revolution of a social body—monarchy, republic, democracy, tyranny, etc.—because it is the loss of the body proper, the geophysical body. For the first time in history, the contraction happened at a *meta-geophysical* level, and not at a sociological, or socio-physical level. And this is unheard of. Speed here is essential. The temporal compression we've talked about before results from the power of instantaneous speed, of interactivity, of feed-back. etc. Therefore we're in front of a situation without reference. It has an astronomical dimension, in the sense that astronomy refers to "revolution." As early as the Roman Empire, as early as the roads and the canals, and then railways and highways, the vocation of technology by virtue of its globalizing dimension was to irrigate the territorial body. Then they irrigated the social body, specifically with electricity and the energy revolution: whence the telephone and everything that has come after it. And the city was the place of this irrigation: the irrigation of the city, but also of the apartment, etc.

And subsequently, technology has taken on the human body itself, the animal body.

The third revolution is about irrigating the human body, first in an external way by means of electronic equipment (see Steve Mann) and then in an internal way by invading the body with flesh-eating prosthetics. I think one can say that with transplant techniques, technology has been inserted inside the body.

That is the first offensive. The next is not penetrating a body which is already there, but constructing one from scratch.

The other aspect is genesis: the possibility of industrializing the living organism, industrializing the species itself.

Artificial Selection

After natural selection (Darwin), and biosocial selection (Galton), we're now getting to the genomic assembly-line.

It will no longer be a question of the eugenics of relative performance or Galton's eugenics of artificial selection (and let me say that Darwin was against Galton). It will be a question of *information selection.*

We need to go back quickly over that history. It is true that Darwin found the theories of Francis Galton, his first cousin, a bit too radical.

Galton advocated taking direct control over human reproduction assuming that all the aptitudes acquired though the "survival of the fittest" and the elimination of the unfit had run their course over time. More urgent measures were now needed to protect "the races best fitted to play their part on the stage of life from being crowded out by the incompetent, the ailing, and the desponding." Evil inheritance, *not education or environment, was the cause of modern degeneration and it had to be weeded out artificially. To this effect, in 1870 Galton founded the science of* Eugenics *(from Greek* eu, *"good," and* genos, *"race") taking as its model the breeding of plants and animals. His project was to raise "the present miserably low standard of the human race to one in which the Utopias in the dreamland of philanthropists may become practical possibilities."*[30] *Unspeakable deeds have been committed in the name of Utopia and Galton's dreams were no exception. As a biosocial science backed up by rudimentary statistics, eugenics sounded rational enough, even altruistic, at least among the better classes: Anglo-Saxon Protestants fearful of the increasing urban squalor and social degeneration brought about by industrialization. The new science of evolutionary advancement actually grew very popular both in Europe and in the United States, where sterilization laws targeting the diseased and the "feebleminded" were enforced in twenty-four states. In 1900 eugenics also received a strong reinforcement from the rediscovery of Gregor Mendel's laws of recombination of hereditary characteristics in plants which identified genes as the single biological determinants. Mendelism in effect put an end to Lamark's long-standing claim for the inheritance of acquired characters. Triumphant on both sides of the Atlantic, the "science for race improvement" only declined precipitously among "democratic" countries after the Nazi state enthusiastically embraced race policies. It is easy to understand why eugenics has been systematically played down ever since as the forerunner of modern human genetics.*

Actually biogenetics now is about moving to a total, to an absolute eugenics, a eugenics of the perfection of creation itself. Here the essential thing would be the *program*, and not the culture. In my opinion, artificial selection and information selection cannot be separated. Behind them there is clearly the idea of a humanity—not to mention a post-humanity—that has been "augmented," as one talks about a reality that has been augmented through cybernetic procedures. In all rigor, one can imagine the creation of human *races*—no longer the human species in the singular, but human species *in the plural*.

Genetic Robots

At this point it would be possible to tamper with the map of the human genome to create not only high performance humans, but also sub-humans.

In my view, we cannot advance the genetic question today without positing the fatal dimension of eugenics. Behind the idea of the super-human, (which is Galton's idea taken up by Mengele), there is inevitably the idea of an inferior race. What people fail to understand is that the prefix "super" includes the under valuation of every other human. As soon as you create the idea of a super-human, you discredit, you downgrade, you degrade a kind of human. Her existence *de facto* decrees that the rest of us are sub-humans. To my mind, by the way, the super-man is a monster too, even if he is perfect. Super-men are like transgenic produce: they will be resistant to everything.

The idea of the sub-human, though, didn't wait for biotechnology. It was already present in colonial times...

To develop this idea further, one could say that mankind today would be the equivalent of the Savage, as compared to the civilized Conquistador. Far away lands would no longer be where one would discover savages, good or bad. Rather, one would find them in a laboratory. In the lab, they would have fabricated a new plural human species. The primate species, the first kind, made from eggs and sperm, would be considered primitive. In super-racism one would find all over again the foundations of both colonialism, racism and xenophobia, but on a cosmic level. Whence the idea that the extra-human is the future of the extra-terrestrial. And that the search for little green men wasn't science fiction, but the forerunner of the search for a superior man. Simply, since nobody dared be part of Nazi eugenics, we went with outer-space and opted for little green men from Mars.

William Burroughs was one of those who saw early on the possibility, in genetic engineering, of bringing about a final ecological leap into space. He estimated that the human species was still in a state of neoteny and was not biologically designed to remain as it is now. Hence the need for an "astral body," a lighter body meant to fulfill our spiritual destiny in space. Science fiction was a pioneer, too.

What frightens me is the idea of genetic robots, living robots, living organisms which have been roboticized through the manipulation of the genetic code.

They wouldn't be industrial robots, but information robots, children of the computer and the human genome.

What is most threatening is a genetic map capable of making a human robot, a living slave—a new form of slavery made possible by genetic engineering. The question of the clone or the chimera reproduces the notion of robotization, but through genetic means. Greg Wenter, for example, claimed a few years ago that life could be created with a mere three hundred genes. And this went a long way to suggest that one would be ready to manufacture a sub-life. It would be primitive, but it would work.

Since then, of course, scientists have been floating the idea of producing acephalic monsters from embryonic stem cells, human bodies without a forebrain that would be kept alive in order to become a fresh source of organs.

Sub-humans, that world misfortune created in colonial times, were not programmed in a factory. Whereas, in this case, with the modification of the genome, it would be an industrial program, as in *Terminator*. The whole question of the control of the living organism has to do with the contraception of the human species. This is not contraception preventing the birth of a man or woman; or contrarily, this is not the absence of birth. No. It is the possibility of an extinction, not to say extermination, of the human species in the singular.

Super-Racism

And that raises the question of racism anew...

Or rather of *super-racism*. What is racism? Racism posits that there are "superior" and "inferior" races within the singleness of the human species. The biggest racist in the world recognizes that. Even the degraded are degraded within this unity. The racist calls them "inferior," but they still are human. Through all its massacres, its monstrosities and its horrors, racism remains within the unity of the human species and is relative to this unity.

This is also the claim that Robert Antelme made in The Human Race, *the French classic of the camps on par with Primo Levi's* Survival in Auschwitz. *Antelme, a resistant sent to a forced labor kommando in 1944, kept insisting that "the distance separating us from another species is still intact." There could only be one human race, not several. "No one could at will join or leave the human species, or force anyone to become an animal or a tree."*[31] *But this emphatic denial confirmed the real nature of the Nazi project: beyond exterminating them, it was the existence of the Jews and Gypsies* as humans *that they attempted to eradicate.*

The question of multiplying human species has never been raised before. The racist was preserved from this excess by the fact that there was only one human species, and different races. What I am saying is that the *genetic bomb* now risks exploding this unity.

But wasn't it already exploded in the camps? As early as in 1933, Georges Bataille explored this idea in a short essay on "abjection" where he suggested that humans would turn into vermin *if they were not in a position to resist the "imperative gesture" that reduced them to objects. The exclusion of "abject forms" took away from them any value as humans and turned them into things. The concept of "abjection" (mostly in terms of borderline subjectivity) gained a lot of currency in the United States after the publication of Julia Kristeva's essay on Celine,*[32] *but nobody seemed to realize how topical this analysis had been at the time: it foreshadowed the experiments in the camps. Giorgio Agamben unwittingly touched upon this question in* Homo Sacer *when he examined the fate of "Musselmen" in the camps*[33]—

people who lost their will to live and any survival instinct in response to extreme conditions—and concluded that "life stripped bare" transformed politics into bio-politics. But precisely: the S.S. didn't yet have the kind of bio-technology that we know, yet they began enforcing their policy biologically by transforming the nature of bodies in the camps and treating the deported like sub-humans.

They opened the Gates of Hell.

In his book Nazi Medicine and Its Victims, *Ernst Klee cited the account of a prisoner in a camp who witnessed "a kind of exhibition of flesh" prior to the executions of a group of Jews.*[34] *Like "horse dealers," he wrote, the S.S. doctors felt the thighs and calves of the men and women lined up before them and chose in advance "the best pieces." Then they made a "human stew" with them to farm bacteria in the lab.*

This is horrible. And yet with the possibility of multiplying human species, racism will become exponential.

Auschwitz-Birkenau

Now bio-genetics works at a molecular level, with "living material," doing away with conventional racial distinctions. What could be exponential then is that, paradoxically, what we would have is a racism without races. *This wouldn't prevent, of course, bio-genetics from creating* races of every kind genetically both within and without the human race.

A racism beyond the human race is something unthinkable, but it will make it necessary to think the unthinkable, that is, to make the jump beyond ethics. And we know that they made the jump at Auschwitz. In my opinion, Mengele is a figure who has been obscured by those who have sponsored him, the big pharmaceutical labs. Ernst Klee's book is truly important if you want to see what an enigma we are faced with. Mengele goes back to Galton. There's an Anglo-Saxon, a Darwinian dimension to him by virtue of his technical culture, his biotechnology, and his work on twins.

Mengele had been transferred from Berlin to Auschwitz because of the "unique possibility" this would give him to conduct racial biological research there. He kept sending "human material" to his boss, Pr. Von Verschuer, director of the Kaiser Wilhelm Institute, for his research on the Mendelian laws of inheritance. They included boxes packed with pairs of heterochromatic eyes extracted from Gypsies that he killed himself, and dissection of twins he infected with typhus. (Mandel assumed that physical characters like eye colors or diseases could be passed on unchanged through single genes over several generations). The purpose was to create a "central collection in hereditary biology."

Mengele's experiments were used again. These are the obscure origins of biotechnologies

We may not realize yet that the world is in the process of becoming Nazi in a new way.

We are witnessing what Bernard Chouraki the other day called "a planetary Shoah." Because Auschwitz-Birkenau—the S.S. laboratories were in Birkenau—was the anticipation of what is happening today with transgenics. The extermination camps— not the concentration camps, they had those in Australia for the indigenous peoples—were the biggest genetic laboratories of the period. The whole enterprise enriched the big pharmaceutical labs and enriched science itself.

Mass Killers

Eugenics thrived in the United States after the turn of the century and this went on well into World War II. Visiting the Kaiser Wilhelm Institute in 1940, T.U.V. Ellinger, a well-known American geneticist, compared the German project of eliminating Jewish "inferior hereditary attributes" to the American treatment of the black population.[35] *Actually the American science of eugenics was the model for Nazi doctors, a fact that was quickly forgotten in the US. It was, of course, easier to demonize the Nazis.*

Mengele is the one who dared to take on the mass quantity. It is impossible to deal with these questions without involving the notion of violence. The extermination camps still were a relative dissemination of violence because they were part of the more general violence of Nazism. But they were places inside where violence was concentrated, and these were the laboratories. The camps were not just linked to Nazism, they were experimenting with a new kind of violence, and this violence has never abated. You can find it in snuff films for instance, or among *mass killers*, an aspect I developed in *A Panorama of Events.*[36] When I say "mass killer," I am talking about *Rambo* the film. For me, Rambo is an archetype, like Antigone, Don Quixote, Hamlet. It goes hand in hand with the Mass Killer. Rambo is the patriotic apotheosis of the Mass Killer.

There's a violence in concentration.

Concentration is a lot like violence. A term is emerging now in France that refers to violence in closed environments. When a man attacks another man or woman in the street, we call him a thief or a rapist. But when men gather in a parking lot or in a cellar to rape a woman, we are dealing with "concentrated violence." Group violence needs concentration, not only a concentration of persons, but also concentration in space.

The Australians call gang rapes, "pack rapes." Pack is a word that's used for dogs, but also for "cramming things together."

The pack again. We are faced with a "package" of violence, and that can only lead to death. The very moment of concentration is a movement to the limit.

We talked earlier about globalization being a contraction of the world, a temporal compression that made the world exiguous. This may account as well for the increasing violence that we're witnessing everywhere. The theorists of crowds. Sorel, Gustave Le Bon, McDougall already sensed as much early in the century. People were flooding from the countryside into the cities and disorder was threatening to get out of hand…

Absolutely, concentration…

Urban masses reminded them of the French Revolution, furious, disorganized, uncontrollable crowds, the enragés. *Even Freud, in* Group Psychology and the Ego, *written after the First World War, wasted no time in saying: we need fathers, leaders to check the threat of violence. The masses needed a totem. Mussolini was just coming to power in Italy, concentration camps weren't too far off…*

Mengele relied on concentration and mass effect. He is the one who brought this to fruition in the camps. I recall they did concrete experiments on submersion in cold water for the pilots who were falling in the North Sea. Many Luftwaffe pilots used to humanitarian ends what had been tested in the bathtubs in the camps, and the same goes for the Wehrmarcht. It is certain that these horrible experiments—and in the camps we can use the term *human experiments*—had practical applications that no one ever talks about...

Human Experiments

Ernst Klee also provided a brief classification of the different types of human experiments conducted by the Wehrmacht: ballistic tests (exploding bullets on the heads of human subjects); administering sulfic acids, or more generally "combat substances" to women in Ravensbruck; injecting gasoline in the body; experimenting with burns; simulating sicknesses like jaundice through injection of picric acid; live vivisection; experiments on children in low pressure chambers, etc. Most of the human guinea-pigs died from these experiments. Many of the Nazi doctors who participated in them, on the other hand, had brilliant careers after the war. We always talk about Nazi biology and Nazi biologists, but Nazi knowledge is rarely presented or acknowledged as such.

Our friend Gérard Rabinowitz, a few years ago, published an article in a well-known Jewish journal, in which he wrote that we mustn't think the Nazis were stupid. And they censored the remark. But the Nazis had an extraordinary intelligence, of course. That's what evil is.

German science after the war was not especially brilliant.

They were all exported, like von Braun... In any case, it's not about limiting this to Germany: Germany, in the field of eugenics, was the explosion of what had begun elsewhere, in the United States and the Nordic countries, not to mention the great French eugenicist...

Alexis Carel...

Yes.

A 1912 Nobel Prize in Medicine, he invented techniques that made organ transplantation possible. He built a glass heart and kept organs removed from animals alive for a significant amount of time. He also happened to admire the Nazis, like his friend Charles Lindbergh, and this eventually made him less attractive in the US.

Teratology

Carel was still a big shot after the war. The question of eugenics today has been obscured because genetics is becoming a cornerstone for the big multinational and bio-technological firms. We can indeed wonder whether it still is genetics, or still a science. Is it part of physics? Is it part of medicine, or bio-physics? Or is it an art? If we answer that it is an art, then we entertain the possibility of creating different kinds, that is, styles, styles of life, *life*-styles. I use the term because art history ("history" in quotation marks) is the life of styles—Impressionism, Cubism, Modernism, Postmodernism, whatever you like. That's why I say that biology is becoming a teratology. The creation of monsters is a *project*, it's not simply an excess. Then teratology will become an expressionist form of art, of science as art, of genetic science as art. It is the freedom of expression of every kind, exactly as in Picasso's work. Whence the idea that in laboratories one would create—I'm exaggerating—Pointillist, Cubist living beings, all the way to genetic operas. In other words, something from fashion. Fashion is becoming a living phenomenon, and we know that fashion goes out of fashion. Here we are touching on the mutation of humankind. We have already seen it in the research on cow ova, that is, the centaur or the Minotaur.[37]

They already have gone pretty far by grafting a human ear on the back of a mouse, or producing "Arnold Schwarzenneger pigs" with chicken genes, not to mention headless mice and tadpoles. (Researchers in Texas deleted the gene that produces the head in the embryo). This is the "artistic" side of genetics. Actually science already seems far ahead of art. And if this kind of experimentation is possible, there is no doubt that it is being pursued right now somewhere.

I am sure of it. They have pummeled us long enough with the story of flying saucers in Area 51 in Nevada, where you went. I mean, it is astonishing to see it again today, after all these decades. They are pulling the little green men from outer space on us, while we know very well that right now they are in the process of working in the labs just about everywhere...

The aliens are among us...

Who would dare claim that hybrids and human cloning have not begun? When you see what America did—I say America, but I could just as well say France—radiating their own citizens to test

115

the atomic bomb, who would believe forty years later that none of this can happen again?

The "laboratories at Auschwitz" were already a form of war, but a war against humanity. A war rerouted via science. And science is still at war. As Mengele told his assistant: "My friend, this will go on and on and on."

If it weren't for eugenics, the "superior" race, Auschwitz and the rest behind these new genetic practices, we could do without asking ourselves: *How far, to what point?* When we say "how far" today, it means: all the way to Auschwitz. It means going all the way. It's thumbs down for the gladiator.

The Art of the Camps

Genetics no longer recognizes the cruelty it is coming from, and that may be what is most dangerous about it: that it may become an ordinary cruelty, a cruelty that we would no longer be capable of recognizing or representing as such.

Not great massacres, the banality of evil.

This project was started in Auschwitz-Birkenau. It could be called the art of the camps.

Yes, a terrorist dimension of art already existed in embryo in fascism. The explicit goal of Josef Mengele, the kind of "body-art" that he practiced, was based on the idea of making the human race a superior esthetic object. One cannot look at the camps without thinking of their esthetic dimension. This esthetic dimension was deliberate, it was part of the cult of the Aryan.

116

Aryan art was displayed openly. It was monumental, neo-classical, sublimated. But this other kind of art practiced by the S.S. in their labs remained secret. And we should put the two together if we want to know what Nazi esthetics really was about.

The development of research on humans today leads no longer to experiments on humans, to human experimentation, as was the case with the Mengele twins, but to *human-experiments.* The freedom of expression to produce human beings, to *create* them, no longer to procreate them. Here we see the religious dimension, the deification of the scientist, the demiurgic impulse: re-fabricating the living. Science has become art. There is an art of science which is the end of science, and maybe the end of art. Because the day when these stylistic expressions are connected to biological creation, out of living materials, then clearly art will stop and science will become demiurgic. Thus humankind would no longer be singular. It would become the product of a creator. But this time, it would no longer be the Creator who is the cause. It would no longer be monotheism, it would be polytheism, except that the creators would be companies. Monsanto, or Novartis would do the programming... I believe that we are leaving biology behind to enter the realm of teratology, that is, the creation of monsters.

Monsters that would be human...

Monsters that would be human, that would be living organisms. What characterizes art is creation. Sacred art idealized it. What is sacred art? It officialized the demiurgic impulse. Today this impulse is no longer sacred, it is profane. And ultimately the problem is no longer the profane body, it is the body which has been profaned.

117

The profaned body finds the sacred through the *homo sacer* and the sacrifice. In my opinion, the demiurgic impulse of sacred art has moved into genetic art, and into other sectors as well.

Body-Art

For the last two decades, representations of the body, fragmented, abject, grotesque, sublime, monstrous, have proliferated in galleries and museums throughout the world, often under the cover of gender studies or psychoanalysis. That kind of inflation appears to me less a return of something that has been "repressed" than a massive symptom of the body's increasing disappearance. It's something like the last fireworks for an endangered entity.

Looking at body-art today, looking at the research being done on the human genome, we cannot forget that we are on the verge of a transgenic art—an art of beings, an art of the bio-techno, and no longer an art of fixed, pictorial forms. This was Mengele's dream—to have biology become an art, and not just an art of biology—a teratology, the art of creating monsters. When you see that people want at all cost to clone a human being, you realize that we are faced with something that is no longer artistic genius, but *genetic engineering*. So now you get some body artists who volunteer to transform themselves, like Orlan and my friend Stelarc, the two best-known body artists, the duo.

You said my friend Stelarc, but you don't seem to agree with him at all.

No, we are totally opposed, but he is incredibly intelligent and I was very proud when he came for the ceremony in which I was nominated Emeritus Professor at the Ecole Spéciale d'Architecture. Stelarc also is a futurist. He said that the human body as it is now will not be able to attain the universe. He and others have this idea that humanity, to survive, has to mutate but mutate voluntarily by its own means. Behind Stelarc then, you have the idea of the cosmonaut, the idea which Jean-François Lyotard also deals with in *The Unhuman*.[38] Inhumanity, actually, also comes about as a consequence of having acquired escape velocity, and with this freedom, we became astronauts or cosmonauts. From that point on, like divers to extreme depths, we can't survive without modifications to our organism. The conquest of space is also a decorporealization of the body, the earth's body and the human body, the world proper and the body proper. This, I think, is one of the big questions of ecology. Ecology has not yet touched on it, it hasn't made much progress there. But it opens something which has more to do with the human than the extra-human.

And then there is Orlan tampering with her own body.

Many years before her physical transformations, Orlan invited me to her studio—it was behind la Coupole—to show me some of her photo-montages and installations (in which, as if by accident, she figured the Virgin, the Madonna, and they were baroque, too). Then at the end of the visit she told me that she was going to have some esthetic surgery done. She asked me: "What do you think?" I told her I wasn't in favor of it. I didn't think putting her own physical integrity at risk was such a good idea. And she answered: "I'm free." The artist must have the freedom of expression. So I said: "Listen, Orlan, you are free to do whatever you want, even commit suicide. Anyone can commit suicide, all you need is a window. But I am not free to tell you, go ahead. You see what I mean?" She didn't get it. And that's intolerance. For me, the moment you have the right to say: "Go ahead," it's torture, it's in cold-blood. Now they are talking about the French generals who tortured prisoners in Algeria and bragged about it to the papers and in their books.[39] And there are strange things in art history, too. The other day I met a professor of contemporary art history who teaches in a grammar school, and he told me: "When I get to self-mutilation, I'm at a loss to teach it..."

We can go back to the traces of mutilated hands on the walls of prehistoric caves...

Sure, but I can't tell kids: "Take this razor blade, and go for it."

Of course not. I sometimes teach the Marquis de Sade. And then there is Van Gogh ...

Van Gogh was free to commit suicide, to mutilate himself. But that just isn't taught. History says: "*You* are free, but I am not free to..." Because then the torturer has won. The transformation of the living organism into art is unconceivable *because we can't go back*. It's not a disguise or movie make-up, it's a real transformation. And this transformation of the body necessarily sets eugenics in motion. Even if Orlan and the others are not eugenicists, they are leading us down that road. So though Orlan is her own guinea-pig, and is becoming the subject and object of her art, still she opens the door for all the Mengeles to come.

Extreme Sciences

But is it not better opening the door before throngs of little Mengeles rush through it? Jacques Lacan used to say that Charcot's hysterics raised questions to the medical establishment with their bodies, the way one raises a question mark with a pen. Is it not better to provoke a reflection publicly on what is happening to the body now than be confronted with a fait accompli? *Orlan is mostly known, of course, for the implants she had inserted in her temples, but a case could be made that she is doing exactly* what you're doing, *upping the ante on bio-technology and exposing in advance, in her flesh, the dizzying transformations that are in the offing. Obviously she is also making them acceptable by presenting her performances as "interventions" (in the surgical sense) and the operating room as an "operating theater," probably in reference to Artaud. But can art still have a prophetic function when it is coming at the end of art and at the beginning of techno-science, merging presentation with representation?*

To go from representation to presentation is to lose distance. It's this kind of leveling that is now occurring with the pollution of distances in the world. The last art is art that takes matter as its material—matter in the broadest sense, not pigment. We're witnessing a *land art* that has become generalized.

It's the collapse of the animal body and the territorial body. This is the essence of the myth.

Land art is basically matter. Artistic matter is no longer painting, sculpture, architecture, engraving, or colors and pigments; it's the living organism itself. The question is again: to what point?

This is the problem of limits. Are there explicit rules in the extreme sciences, *as in extreme sports? And what is it that makes us call them "extreme"? It seems to indicate that we don't abide by strict safety measures, that we foresee the possibility of accidents, of spinouts that could lead to injury, mutilation, or even death. And that we are ready to accept the consequences, whatever they are. The concentration camps were extreme experiments too, except that they were imposed on the prisoners, with death the explicit outcome. It wasn't a public spectacle like Roman games and circuses, to the contrary the Nazis kept them secret.*

In Roman times the circus was a practice that was culturally accepted, whereas everyone now would contest that as a crime against humanity.

In extreme sports, at least you know ahead of time that the limits have been removed or suspended. Then you can still use caution, cut your losses. The worst is when you no longer realize that you have crossed the limit, or even worse: that there are no more limits. The conjunction of science with the living organism leads to an extreme art, or an art of the extreme, or even an extreme that no longer has anything to do with art...

We are always on the edge. Art is *polluting* itself. So you have the teratology of pollution. Electromagnetic pollution, chemical pollution, the pollution of the water and the air are all a form of art—expressionist art, but a form of art.

But didn't we already cross the threshold? We're already engaged in this paradigm in all sorts of ways. We intervene in the body with drugs, prostheses, implants, or we modify it with plastic surgery.

The notion of personal identity or even the identity of the species is becoming more and more uncertain. Transformational mechanisms are at work everywhere you look... Infligen, a bio-tech company in Wisconsin, has cloned calves which are part-human since human DNA was added to their genetic make-up in order to produce human protein in their milk. Many other products and organs for humans are just about to be farmed that way. Fukuyama himself warned that we're already mixing human genes with so many other species that it will become increasingly difficult to know what a human being is.[40] *Extremes are commonplace even in art terms. I met a young French artist, Anne Esperet, who is dabbling with self-eugenics and considers technological manipulations of the body to be an alternative utopia, an attempt to anticipate individual genetic choices through a kind of exploratory forward flight, just like Orlan's work. So she contacted slaughter-houses and chose the parts to be cut out of pigs, cattle, etc. Then she electronically recomposed monstrous anthropological configurations with pieces of lung, etc. Her "bio-fictional" images are sometimes unsettling, to say the least, but sometimes they simply look like comic strips, big blue veal eyes floating over various pieces of animal anatomies...*

I find it terrifying. It's a sign of the art of abjection,

Abjection

Contrary to those American artists in the eighties who tried their hands at " abject art" and ended up objectifying *the abject by mimicking certain repulsive substances, excrement, etc., Esperet's kind of "portraits" mostly don't not come off that way. They are colorful, brash, pastel pink, a kind of parody of themselves and of actual monstrosities to come.*

Yes, but there is no art without the practice, and the practice of cutting pure bodies to recompose them...

It's impossible, obviously, not to flash on what preceded it, the "human crafts" in the camps, with tattooed skin stretched on lines like laundry, waiting to be turned into "gift items," as the human skulls, shrunken heads or varnished organs meant to adorn S.S. officers' desks. Actually all these "objects" were exhibited outdoors by the US army when they liberated Buchenwald. . The first "art museum" in a camp.

It makes me think of Dr. Gunther von Hagens' exhibit of laboratory cadavers in Mannheim in 1997. What he is doing follows the same logic. He presented plasticized bodies,[41] cadavers of living beings sculpted in a surrealist manner. It caused practically no problem, and yet von Hagens did this in Germany, and in the "Museum of Work" to boot, which is a little much. This indicates that, given the chance, laboratories tomorrow will genetically program beings, different human species, *avant-garde* species, so to speak.

During the Baroque period, displaying bodies was both artistic and clinical. I'm afraid it may all eventually turn into a "freak show." Already anyone can take a three dimensional CD cruise through the inside of a dead body sliced with a laser into one-millimeter.[42] Science and art now have a tendancy to merge with entertainment.

In my opinion, if you look at what is happening in contemporary art, they are on the verge of considering genetics and cloning to be a form of art. That is, a form of "free expression." But where does the liberty of expression stop in the realm of the sciences? If it doesn't stop, Mengele will be a prophet...

Transgenic art

For a few years now biological art has been developing a culture of art. I use "culture" here in the biological sense, like the culture of bacteria. You know Eduardo Kac, the Brazilian artist ...

The transgenic rabbit...

Yes, the creator of Alba, the Green Fluorescent Protein (GFP) Bunny. Before that Kac created a fluorescent dog whose social integration (it was part of the project) raised a few hairy ethical questions. His most recent creation was "The Eighth Day," which claims, I guess, to improve on the Seventh. It brought together, under the aegis of art, a biological robot connected to the internet, a few mice and a GFP fish, but also plants and GFP amoebas—a whole diminutive universe based on the direct manipulation of living organisms. Biological art, though, often does not work on the living being itself, but on the mechanisms of life, and some of these projects appear to be much closer to science than to art. Take Michael Punt, one of these sorcerer-apprentices. He has created "artistic entities that are half-alive" by transmitting electric impulses from a fish neuron onto a computer program ("Fish and Chips"). Another "apprentist" Paul Perry, combined a white blood cell from his own blood with a cancerous mouse cell in order to obtain what he calls the "Hybridome," a new immortal cell.[43] These experiments have nothing to do with what we usually call "art," although maybe it doesn't make much sense to maintain this kind of distinction—art at this point—being simply what is exhibited as art. In any case, transgenic art is now being added to the other arts and seems poised to become an "augmented" art, the way reality is being "augmented" by cybernetic procedures.

Reinventing Myths

No, that's what people think, but really transgenic art is renewing the other arts from the inside. Because its focus is the map of the human genome. And we can't treat genetic science as just another science in parallel with the others. It is inside all the other sciences. It is a way to focus science on its source—the living organism and the knowledge of it. In this sense, it is a snake swallowing its tail. Science is becoming myth again. Instead of enhancing reason, it is welcoming unreason and magic, a factory for anything at all: the demiurgic, centaurs... Alchemists helped originate science, and then we moved beyond alchemy...

By means of science...

Experimental science is the opposite of storytelling, chimera and myths. The rational position of science had freed itself little by little from alchemy and magic. But now knowledge has been mortally wounded. Instead of opposing the alchemist, the scientist is becoming an alchemist again. It is the idolatry of calculation, the idolatry of the genetic bomb, that has brought us back to alchemy. So, to say that the transgenic art is an art like the others—it's not, because it exterminates the *source* of the other arts. The living organism is irreplaceable. The living organism is not of the same nature as what produces it. Right now the scientist is saying: "Yes, but the living organism has been surpassed." So, I say: "Alright, then we are encroaching on the demiurgic, we are coming back to the great myths." Science is reinventing myths. And the delirium starts over.

But maybe it never stopped doing that. The invention of the objectivity of science itself was a myth.

What I'm trying to say is that today calculation is leading us back to the chimera and the myth of the super-human. Not Nietzsche's super-man, but the super-man of teratology.

You called the genetic sterilization of semen "necro-technology." The paradox is that the theory of the "superior race" would have in fact led to a kind of internal devastation, the obsolescence of the blond Aryan, the way monoculture depletes the genetic reserves and diminishes the capacity of plants to resist disease.

And Aryans would have been eliminated. Monoculture is the end of biodiversity. So you get the Monsanto research. What happened to the Cambodians would have happened to the Germans. What was really extraordinary about the small area of Cambodia is the self-elimination, the suicide of the nation itself. It was not simply the Reign of Terror—they decapitated everyone and in the end the executioners also went to the guillotine (that happened to Louis XVI at the Place de la Concorde, a primordial image for the French). In Cambodia they did this on the scale of one or two million people. If the Vietnamese hadn't showed up, there wouldn't have been any Cambodian left. I am convinced that the Germans would have done the same if they had won the war. They began by getting rid of the Gypsies, homosexuals, Jews, etc. Afterward, they would have got rid of Germans who wear glasses, or who have long hair, or whatever.

That's part of the suicidal state *syndrome.*

They started up an extermination machine, and this machine is still running.

Euthanasia, Anesthesia

At the same time, mass extermination was still at the cottage industry stage. This is obvious in Cambodia, where the Khmer Rouge emptied the cities and refused to have anything to do with technological culture, but it is also true of the Nazi camps, which were still very far from today's capacity for experimentation and annihilation. Actually it is only recently that IBM's crucial contribution to the programming of the sinister trains and the identification of millions of deportees, has come to light. The S.S. relied so much on the IBM programs to do the job that they paid their bills to IBM all the way until the bitter end. But for the most part extermination in the camps was implemented through rather primitive means. What did the S.S. do? They simply did away with everything: they cut off food, sleep, space, dignity, just let everyone rot. You can unplug human beings the same way you unplug a machine in euthanasia. And prisoners became abject even in their own eyes.

The Nazi *euthanasia* began with Nazi *anesthesia*, and that is really important. You can't understand that without Goebbels. Nazism has two key figures, not just one: Hitler *and* Goebbels. Goebbels is the one who anesthetized the State, and after that you can begin the euthanasia of society—those next door and finally one's own people. If German propaganda, the *Propagandastaffel*, had not anesthetized feelings, the extermination would not have been possible. In my view, we have to hold Goebbels at least as responsible (and I mean at least) as Hitler. Goebbels is an extremely important figure. Hitler would never have succeeded without him—well, if you can call it success.

First they had to numb the population.

Right, anesthesia. Euthanasia, amnesia, anesthesia, these are all words very much in the news. These words are once again current, and so is the "Procedure Silence."[44]

There were two kinds of anesthesia in the camps. The first one involved training the S.S. so they would no longer have any human reaction, either to their own death, or to the death of others...

Right, that's the "drilling" of storm troopers. This happens all over the place, too. Alas, it's the soldier. I'll give you a personal example. During the Second World War, my wife was in Angers on the right bank of the Loire, and I was in Nantes on the left bank. This was the front. General Patton had arrived on the Loire, and the Germans were on the other side. So she was among the recently liberated, and I was among the Germans. It lasted for about a month. There were many casualties, bombings, all of it, and she went to help the people in the hospitals. There was an S.S. prisoner, and the Americans had taken him to the hospital for treatment. He was on the verge of dying, and this man refused blood transfusions because he had no way of knowing where the blood came from—and he died.

Apathy

Then there's the other form of "apathy," as the Marquis de Sade used to call it—the deliberate control of their emotions, pathos, by the Libertines—produced by extreme deprivation in the camps, the twilight state of the so-called Musselmen. And there's a strange resonance here between the impassivity of the executioners and the total depletion of affects in their victims, as if this fatal *couple colluded to eradicate between them anything that could be called human. In between these two extremes could be found the peculiar status of those who gradually adapted to the extermination process. The diary of Dr. Johann Paul Kreme I read recently—Kreme was a Nazi doctor in Auschwitz, and not among the worst—is edifying in this respect: an early member of the party, a surgeon and a specialist of the biology of human heredity, Kremer was assigned to Auschwitz-Birkenau in 1941 and stayed there until the very end. A seasoned academic, he didn't go through the S.S. training and his first involvement in the "special actions" in Auschwitz (standing at the infamous ramp and monitoring the gassing that followed) horrified him (Nazi doctors were the ones who stood at the infamous ramp to select the deportees and monitor the gassing) "In comparison," he wrote in his diary, "Dante's* Inferno *seems almost like a comedy. It's not for nothing that Auschwitz is called an extermination camp." For the first fifteen actions he participated in, Kremer witnessed what he called "horrible scenes," which he simply listed among meticulous accounts of his domestic life. And then he stopped mentioning them altogether. In the meantime he had resumed his own research, extracting "live human material" (liver, pancreas, spleen) from sick prisoners assigned to be killed by injection. He also got quite excited over a case-study of tailless cats. The subject of his dissertation, published at the time, was "The Hereditary Transmission of Traumatic Mutilation," a neo-Lamarkian study for which he innocently expected to receive a chair in Human Genetics. It put him instead at odd with his colleagues. Curiously, this rebuff was enough to turn the Nazi doctor against Nazi science, accusing it in his diary of ignoring the freedom of scientific research (!) and bringing him to deny that there existed "an Aryan, negroid or Jewish science, only a true and a false science."[45] This didn't prevent him, of course, from attending the beatings and*

killings of Jewish prisoners and the liquidation of helpless Musselmen.
The uncanny mixture of petty concerns, odd resentment and increasing
insensitivity to the surrounding atrocities goes a long way to validate
Hannah Arendt's judgment on "the banality of evil." This kind of
insensitivity exists as well, in various degrees, among doctors at large.

Cruelty

Yes, medical science does have something to say here. The cool-
headed gaze belonged to doctors and nurses, to those they used
to call the *practicioners of the art* before it belonged to artists.
Doctors believed that this gaze of the surgeon necessarily went
with the job, but at the same time they opened the door to the
cold-blooded gaze of the man who tortures as soon as he puts
on a uniform. Then, little by little, this gaze became the sign of
professionalism. It appeared as a virtue: "He has a cool head."
Whereas prior to the modern period, surgeons, and those who
did research on cadavers, including painters like Leonardo da
Vinci, didn't brag about it, even if they did mention it in their
notebooks. But they couldn't make this cold gaze something
heroic. It was a kind of remorse.

The "clinic" hadn't been born yet, as Foucault would say.

No, it hadn't. All of these things are tied to modernity, they are
tied to electrodes. Today they're talking about "*gegene*" [a form of
torture involving portable electric generators], which was used
during the Algerian War, but before *genene*, there was the research
of that French doctor who put electrodes on the simple-minded
and photographed their spasms—he said he was doing an anato-
my of life, a grammar of expressions.

That was Dr. Duchene analyzing the movements of each facial muscle in 1862. There were electroshock experiments as well in Auschwitz, not just in Rodez. Cruelty wasn't only meant for the stage.

What Artaud translated in his art, he did through pain. In this sense he is both a victim and a forerunner.

Artaud wrote "The Theatre and the Plague" in 1933, the same year as Bataille's notes on Abjection. Bataille was dreaming of sacrifice. Artaud felt the century passing through his body like an electric shock. The brown plague was on its way to infest the entire world.

In my opinion, most artists were in Artaud's situation, the great ones anyway, the ones who revealed it all. Then later we had the exhibitionists. Curiously, the exhibitionists showed up *after* the Second World War. For my money, the Viennese Actionists are exhibitionists who have nothing in common with Artaud or Otto Dix, those who suffered. They're playing with the detachment of a dandy—like the S.S.

Paradoxically, I would also put Marguerite Duras in that category. She was a sacred monster, but not a sacrificial one. She came too late to be a victim. All she managed to do then was exhibit wounds that she had- n't experienced. Which takes a certain courage and recklessness.

There would be much to say on torture as a form, so to speak, of dance, of art, of love, etc. There is material there, not simply con- cerning the Algerian War, but in other fields, too. Laure Adler, Marguerite Duras' biographer, has revealed some things about her that are not so admirable.

There's also her account in The War *of the torture she inflicted on this French informant during the last days of the Liberation of Paris...*

Horrible. Whatever people say, women have not really participated in these horrors. It's pretty rare.

Nietzsche put torture and cruelty at the root of traditional cultures. To behold suffering gives pleasure, he wrote provokingly, but to cause another to suffer affords an even greater pleasure. There is no doubt that the torture Duras inflicted on that French snitch gave her pleasure. The description is eroticized. What is so compelling in the analysis Bataille gives in "Abjection and miserable forms," on the other hand, is precisely that the S.S. didn't eroticize the bodies of their victims.

No, they didn't.

They took no pleasure in it because they didn't consider them as part of the human species. That's what I was trying to say before: genetics may not have existed yet, but already, with the means at hand, the S.S. managed to exclude the Jews from humanity. This is why so many survivors from the death camps, for years, couldn't even speak about their experience. They had been forced into an inhuman condition. Robert Antelme suffered as well, but not in racial terms. And I suspect that his emphatic claim about the unity of the human race has a lot to do with that. Unlike Duras, who was still his wife at the time, he was exposed the horror of the labor camps. And yet he was spared the humiliation of the Jews. Primo Levi, who experienced it, dealt with it instead as a scientist, with the detachment of the observer-participant. Like Simone Weil subjecting herself to the assembly-line, Auschwitz turned Primo Levi into a clinician of malheur.

Hannah Arendt and Simone Weil certainly were more important than people thought. They touched a nerve, they touched deep roots like no one else before them. I can't talk about the camps. I can only talk about the bombings just as well as Alexander Kluge in *The Bombing of Alberstadt*, which is a really great book; or Pynchon in *Gravity's Rainbow*, since I lived through it. I am not what one would call a fanatic of the Apocalypse. It's not my thing. The end of the world doesn't interest me. For me the Apocalypse is just a great literary text. But clearly the twentieth century has an apocalyptic side to it. Hiroshima and Auschwitz are apocalyptic. They are at the limit. This is total delirium, and it is in every way comparable to the frenzy of atomic research. And the search for the genetic bomb is the third bomb.

2. THE ACCIDENT OF SCIENCE

Three Bombs □ Information Chernobyls □ Mutating War □
Unlimited Destructive Force □ Post-humanity □ Accident of
Knowledge □ Positive Negativity □ Militarization of Science □
Artificial Intelligence □ Total Accident [] Very Worst □ Human
is the End □ Knowing the Facts □ Runaway Train □ Imperial
Illusion

Three Bombs

Einstein is the first one who talked about the "genetic bomb."

Yes. Einstein recognized three bombs: the *atomic* bomb, the *cyber*
bomb, and the *genetic* bomb. Alongside Auschwitz and Hiroshima,
the atomic bomb sets off the question of the possible end of the
human species through extinction of a way of life, through pollution of the environment, through radiation poisoning. But the
information bomb was born at the same time—Eniac and calcula-
tors made the atomic bomb possible, and it was the information
bomb that allowed one to decode the encoding of the human
genome map. The atomic bomb has been a frenzy which we have

not been able to leave behind. Then they set off the second frenzy, the cyber bomb, the bomb of information. And now the third bomb which is beginning—the third frenzy. Einstein called it the "demographic" bomb, but it goes without saying that the demographic bomb is no longer simply the bomb of demographics which he imagined in the fifties as a population explosion—that there would be millions and millions of men, and the earth would become uninhabitable. No. Rather, the information bomb is in the process of programming the genetic bomb, that is, the modification of the human species, its plurality, its fractalization. (It is possible to think that this research is in fact being done to counter demographics, that is, to introduce a sub-species and a super-species. But one must hide that because it recalls Auschwitz too much.) The three bombs work together in a relationship of all-out war; they reinforce one another. But in the middle of it all, *it is the information bomb that is knowledge*. It decides. Even if at first the computer was not that important in nuclear physics research—indeed it did not yet exist—we can say that afterwards all the progress in atomic and genetic research were made thanks to the computer, thanks to the calculation speed of machines massively grouped in parallel. We are thus faced with the realization of what Einstein was saying, except that the demographic bomb has become the genetic bomb. But isn't this genetic bomb a means to combat the overpopulation of these primitive men who are reproducing like rabbits? Are not the atomic bomb and the genetic bomb the equivalent of an extermination of the primate human species, the one that reproduces by means of blood and sperm? Does this not promote a super-humanity that has been "improved," a eugenic humanity, by virtue of the decoding of the genome? If one manages to discredit the population explosion, clearly the relationship to procreation is going to change.

People can't be allowed to multiply at will...

No, sir.

Some control must be exercised over births, or certain births: repro-duction by science and disqualification of natural birth. This is already implied in the phenomenon of sexuality at a distance.

I said that tele-sexuality is the universal condom. It's interactivity.

Information Chernobyls

Unreal sex in real time. This leads us back to the information bomb. Is that an apocalyptic bomb as well?

Let's just say that right now the information bomb is in the process of revealing its explosive power in the interventions made on behalf of those sites attacked by viruses: the "Melissa" virus and then the "I Love You" virus. So, I feel like saying that the information bomb has entered reality. Five years ago I said that we were heading towards information Chernobyls. An information Chernobyl has already taken place: "I Love You" is an information Chernobyl. They are talking about a five bil-lion dollar loss, and maybe twice that. "Melissa," I believe, cost one hundred sixty million dollars; it didn't get very far. There is a crescendo effect and this is the proof that cybernetics has an explosive force. It is the possibility of creating an acci-dent at the very same instant, or almost, on a worldwide scale. Cybernetics is indeed a bomb. But it does not at all resemble traditional weapons of mass destruction, whether molecular or nuclear.

In Kosovo, in Iraq, war was mostly being waged by means of electronic jamming...

Yes, electronic counter-measures.

It was multi-media warfare.

And all the more so that war is no longer tied to a declaration of war because it is no longer tied to any territory whatsoever. For there to be a declaration of war, nations must be juxtaposed. Some kind of succession must exist: a state of peace, a state of war, an armistice, an intermission between acts of the play. As soon as we enter interactivity, there is no more before and after—there is only *during*. And the duration has the speed of a lightning bolt. So we are indeed faced with the possibility of a new war, a cybernetic war that has nothing to do with traditional weaponry. Moreover the destruction of Milosevic's forces by the U.S. airforce was insignificant. The U.S. Airforce destroyed the countryside, bridges, electric power plants, etc., but according to these figures provided by NATO, they destroyed only thirteen tanks, twenty tank transporters, and some fifty or so vehicles—all that for a bombardment that lasted seventy-eight days with one thousand sorties—four hundred in the beginning and one thousand in the end... This is totally ridiculous when one has lived through WWII, as you and I have. So I come back to the point: the Gulf War was already the disqualification of military movement. One cannot say that it was a real war. In the war in Kosovo, we didn't even put one man on the ground. As far as the bombing campaign goes, they managed to hit some fixed objects—but that's pretty simple. On the other hand, the enemy was virtually untouched.

Milosevic surrendered because he was alone against the whole world, but he was not compelled by force. So we find ourselves faced with situations that have mutated considerably.

There still were massacres, but they were not due to the actual warfare.

Of course not. It was the knife.

Mutating War

And those who were massacred were the population.

In the First World War, there were six million casualties. In the Second World War, there were sixty million. The percentage of civilians killed is increasing. War is totally mutated, mutating. And the war in Kosovo was the last war of an era. Not simply of a century, but an era of armament. Whence the missile and anti-missile research, all that stuff.

The "I Love You" virus was a declaration of war without a war...

It is but the beginning of a long series of accidents that will most likely call the whole internet into question.

The internet was military in its origin. Wasn't the web meant to protect the communications system in case of an atomic explosion?

The internet is Arpa-net. And Arpa-net was designed to maintain communications that are centralized in military staff headquarters via satellite, or via data bases when faced with the effects of nuclear explosions. It was a relay in the event of the destruction of the large traditional networks, the big antennae. Quite early they realized that the detonation of a powerful atomic bomb in the atmosphere not only contaminated the layers of the atmosphere, but also interrupted radio waves and other forms of communication. The network was centralized before, quite well protected actually at the level of encryption, at the level of entrances and exits, but wanting to protect themselves from electromagnetic explosions, from what they call the EMP effect (electromagnetic pulse effect), they created a random network, with multiple entry points, with all the problems of chaos. On this level, Arpa-net is responsible for our entry into a world of new logic. Still, the bomb must be exploded not too far away, not on the other side of the world. So the internet was launched—well, Arpa-net: Arpa is the Armament Research Department—to create a replacement structure that was much more supple, the Web: a structure where the connections are multiple, infinite, etc. It is the logic of the network.

It's quite ironical that rhizome anarchy (Deleuze and Guattari's inaugural text[46]) would have become the blue-print for military survival. But everything is always reversible, as in Kafka's "The Burrow": each escape route becomes another threatening entry. Terror also is built into the rhizome.

We've talked about the "politics of the worst," and no one will be able to dispute this title of mine.[47]

The American military command is now envisioning wars that no longer require weaponry to be waged. It is not just that they want to spare personnel. They also are in the process of realizing that war is no longer confined to warfare.

Unlimited Destructive Force

On the other hand, we cannot understand anything about what is happening right now without this situation of extraordinary hyper-violence. In *Procedure Silence*, I cited a phrase by Jonathan Mann, who was in charge of the Organization of Health in the Fight against AIDS. He died in the Swissair flight 111 crash. He said: "We are living in a world that is traversed by an unlimited destructive force." It is an extraordinary sentence and when I read a sentence like that, I tip my hat. Because there is a man who fought. It so happens that his case illustrates the twentieth century.

You often cite phrases of that kind at very precise moments, in critical moments, as though they said everything.

Yes, it's really important. They are images. They replace all sorts of analyses. I'm an old painter, you see. I don't just do theory, I make images when I write. I work with images, with the analogon. That's a fact.

You believe in the analog, in the image, not in the machine of vision.

Oh no, I am a man of the analog. I am not a man of the numerolog or the digitalog. Digital technology is like the icing on the cake. It is the completion of everything—in the same way that the genetic bomb closes the system of the three bombs. Thanks to information technology, thanks to calculation, we are replacing the sensations. We are faced with the reconstruction of the phenomenology of perception according to the machine. And this is a catastrophic event.

Back to the destructive force.

Indeed, we have come back to it, but I confess that I used Mann's phrase as an epigraph because I have the feeling that the power of extermination henceforth is the exterminating power of techno-science. Now, of course, there is no Goebbels, there is no Hitler—not yet, and perhaps there will be none.

The capacity for destruction is there. And it comes from the cyber bomb.

What is the information bomb? It is the bomb of science. Because if one leaves the term information aside and replaces it with knowledge, one realizes that the militarization of knowledge is a phenomenon without equal. The war of knowledge— the fact of transforming knowledge into a war-machine by virtue of the speed of estimation, reaction and calculation, is a phenomenon that destroys science. To speak in the broadest terms, science has always been philo-physical. It was philosophico-physical or philosophico-physiological. It was proper to mankind, whether we like it or not. But that is precisely what is in the process of being exploded. Our science is no longer philosophico-physiological.

Post-Humanity

What you're saying is that science is running amok.

Early science was a knowledge that developed in parallel with both philosophy and religion—look at Galileo's trial. We have been pretty well occupied since with eliminating philosophy and religious wisdom. What is scandalous in Galileo's trial is not the trial itself: on the contrary, the trial is quite logical. Everyone recognizes this, even Brecht. What is scandalous is the punishment. Otherwise, why condemn Mengele? Why condemn Pinochet? Why condemn Milosevic, the leader of Serbia?

You mean that it was in keeping with the conceptions of the day to bring Galileo to trial, but that he did not deserve to be punished, whereas it would be scandalous not to condemn Mengele or Milosevic?

What is so bad in Galileo's trial is condemning Galileo. Having brought him to trial is not. Hence this trial was the trial of religion, just as one can say that the trial of Socrates was the trial of political philosophy. However, no political philosophy today is capable of bringing science to trial. Nor is religion powerful enough to bring science to trial. So there is nothing left. Science has become the *deus-ex-machina*. It reigns all powerful. It reigns particularly through its atomic power, and tomorrow through its genetic power, via information technology. Without the information bomb, we would not have the atomic bomb today. We would have only a few simulations of explosions, etc. And without the information bomb, we would not have the genetic bomb, that is, the decoding of the genome map.

Whereas the threats that this bomb poses are explicit.

They are quite clear. A simple example: when Fukuyama launched his idea of a post-humanity, we were right in the middle of the war in Kosovo.

You mean that the war in Kosovo which ostensibly had humanitarian goals, coincided with Fukuyama's assertion that humanity was over?

Let me explain the connection. This war was launched against Milosevic for crimes against humanity. Milosevic was put on trial by the ten allied nations, and we engaged NATO and the entire American bombing force against him. The war in Kosovo was raging, with the air strikes, etc., and at the same moment, quite calmly, an individual announced the end of humanity.

Fukuyama was in fact proclaiming the final victory of liberal democracy over rival ideologies: capitalism allied to "modern natural science" (as Lenin allied Communism with electricity). It was Fukuyama's version of the end of the "big narratives" announced by Lyotard. The question that Fukuyama raised was whether the desire for unequal recognition, which Hegel considered a prerequisite for a livable life, would survive the "universal and homogeneous state" (globalization) anticipated by Alexandre Kojève, or whether it would turn "completely satisfied" citizens into contemptible humans. Peter Sloterdijk, the German philosopher, caused a similar uproar in Germany when he announced the end of the era of humanism and the beginning of the "human park" following the genetic reform of the species' properties. I think that Fukuyama's warning against the coming of a "post-humanity" got a bit confused with all the claims of cyborgs, "post-human" and inhuman that started circulating at the time.

For me the definitive crime against humanity is the possibility that the genetic bomb would take us beyond humanity, that is, snuff it out. But this does not seem to pose a problem for anyone, apart from a few debates, perhaps, in France on Sloterdijk's text, which wasn't very serious.

Accident of Knowledge

In short, we mobilized all the technological might of the West for an operation—the war in Kosovo—that was theoretically conducted against a single man, while it is humanity in its entirety that is being threatened by this same technology...

By knowledge itself, yes. By a knowledge that has been militarized for fifty years.

And this same knowledge allegedly mobilized to protect humanity is in fact in the process of destroying it...

For fifty years now, we have been witnessing the militarization of knowledge—our generation knows it all too well. And not simply with Nobel Prize-winning scientists involved in the Vietnam war, but in every single research. The fruit of this is the three bombs: the atom bomb, the cyber bomb—we know where the internet comes from—and finally the genetic bomb now is in the works: they all are the fruit of this *militarization* of science. That's why I was able to speak of the politics of the worst today with regard to cybernetics.

You think we're heading for catastrophe?

I think the genetic bomb has an apocalyptic dimension to it. Together, moreover, the three bombs have an apocalyptic dimension. Not the end of the world, but extermination in the broad sense.

All this sounds pretty dark.

You know, contrary to what people think of me, I am not a thinker of the excess. I am a lover of extremes. But on the condition of calling extremes extremes, and evil evil. My own inspiration is Carl von Clausewitz, what he calls *going to extremes*. In this Clausewitz has touched on something extraordinary that concerns all humankind, and not simply warfare. So I try to be a kind of periscope of probable catastrophes. What I believe is that these three bombs are developing in parallel. This catastrophic trip-tych is preparing a universal accident, a total accident whose dimension we cannot even imagine. Each time we invent a new technology, whether electronic or biogenetic, we program a new catastrophe and an accident that we cannot imagine. When we invented electricity, we didn't imagine Chernobyl. So, in the research on the living organism, on the "book of life," we cannot imagine the nature of the catastrophe. We can imagine a monster alright, but artists have been imagining that since Breughel and Bosch. Since Bosch, the search and programming for monsters has already taken place. I, for my part, believe that the total cata-strophe which these three bombs are programming is the accident of science. It is no longer science that programs the accidents; it is science that is going to have a permanent accident. You see? *The accident of science is that science is going to destroy itself.* I believe that just as there was an accident of politics, so to speak, in the twentieth century—and what an accident it was, otherwise we would understand nothing about Auschwitz and the Shoah—so at this very moment an accident of science and knowledge is being programmed, whose consequences we cannot imagine. The cyber bomb and the genetic bomb are ripe, as they say, pregnant, both of them, with a scientific catastrophe which we cannot imagine because it is perhaps the catastrophe of science itself. Auschwitz was just a beginning. It was the accident of eugenics.

Everything that is happening right now in genetics has only one reference: it is eugenics.

Positive Negativity

You always say that accidents are positive, because they reveal something that wouldn't have been perceived otherwise. So in a sense Auschwitz is also there to reveal what is the real nature of the genetic bomb.

Accidents always reveal something that is indispensable to knowledge. You can't create the positive without creating the negative. Why do people censure negativity? We should always look for the negative side, including in my own work. Where is Virilio's negativity when he talks about dromology? This would really interest me. That would be a real critique. Negativity is a positive task. For instance I have led a campaign to classify negative objects as "historical monuments.."

The Renault factories, the assembly-lines...

That there are negative monuments for me is an extraordinary advance.

How do you see this negative?

Negative means that we remember in order not to do it again. The pyramids were not preserved to remember the tyrannical character of the Pharaohs who wanted to live forever, but history has been anxious to preserve this memory of Egyptian civilization. As for us, in the twentieth century, we have begun to preserve the concentration camps...If there were no accidents, we couldn't even begin to imagine what the industrial revolution or the revolution in transportation are about. So for me the accident is something like a secular miracle. What is a miracle? It's something that is being given so that one believes, so that there would be a superior hope. In a sense, an accident is a miracle in reverse. Don't forget that my logic of the accident is tied down to Augustine's: when there is no worrying, there is no hope. If we take Auschwitz seriously, beyond all the nihilism, it is the first sign of the Total Accident—of science. It is not just an accident of morality and civilization, no: it is an accident that had a scientific basis. In my view, we have not gone beyond it. On the contrary, we are coming back to it because what is happening right now in genetics is its continuation.

The Shoah wasn't a break in history, an event separating us from everything that went before, to the contrary: it showed the way...

It was a prefiguration. The Shoah is not an end but the beginning. On this account it is very different from communism. Nazism, unfortunately, still has a future while communism doesn't. Indeed there's a tragic fate of fascism, the one that involves science. Not simply the fascism of Aryans, of the S.S., of Goebbels, of Hitler—*the fascism of laboratories*. Here we have reached a limit. Furthermore, we are confronted by limits. There are definitive "limits" in the geometrical sense of the word, not "ends" in the historical sense. We are like goldfish up against the fishbowl. We are looking through the glass, and we have no way of going beyond it. For the moment this is where we are. We're like up against the wall. Already the twentieth century is past, over. We're heading towards the unknown, towards a world that has no history. All the bases for interpretation are insufficient, not only critical sociology, or psychoanalysis, or Marxism, obviously. We're entering a world devoid of cognitive interpretation, without references that would allow us to interpret what is emerging in peace, in war, in politics, in the universe, including in genetics, which is about to replace atomic science and become the major science in the coming century. We're entering the black hole.

Militarization of Science

Science no longer has any limit.

It no longer has any ethical or even any physical limit. It is even attempting to become automated by means of artificial intelligence. We are standing before a phenomenon without equal, one which puts an end to the philosophical aspect of science. And science was not philosophical in the banal sense of the word, but fundamentally so.

Science was grounded in philosophy. It was the cogito. *Existence and reality were founded on reflection.*

But this is precisely what is now being automated. And when the Pope says: "We are witnessing the militarization of science," it means that we are witnessing the end of science. The end of science does not mean that it will stop, or that we are going back to the wheelbarrow. No. It means that we are entering a post-scientific era. Techno-science is post-scientific. And the information bomb is its means, its absolute weapon.

It's become a posthumous science. It didn't survive to itself.

It's a posthumous science. And all this, alas, confirms my ideas, since speed is more important than time. When one looks at Saint-Augustine's philosophy and Heidegger's philosophy, each with respect to their conception of time—I don't see the progress. I mean, really, it is not much when compared to the considerable progress that has been made in other domains. It seems to me that speed has changed everything. We have made progress in the order of speed and at every level of speed. At every level—not simply calculation, knowledge, transmission, but transportation, etc. And that exploded the philo-physical nucleus. So we could say that speed is aging the world. Speed is wearing out the world. Speed is the exhaustion of the world. We are coming back to confinement. We are coming back to enclosure and incarceration. And also exclusion. Whence the escape velocity which offers us a way out, but *a way out to nothing*. To emptiness and the black hole. There is no light outside the atmosphere.

Artificial Intelligence

Is the automation of intelligence also a relationship to speed? Or is it merely a prosthesis?

We have gone from reflection to reflex. When a situation is accelerated, one does not reflect. One has a reflex reaction. Acceleration and speed, not only in calculation, but in the assessment and decision of human actions, have caused us to lose what is time proper, the time for conception, the time for reflection. We enter into a feedback loop. Without an interface, either. When we drive faster than one hundred and seventy miles per hour, we are no longer ourselves. We are plugged in. It is no longer a philosophical, reflective activity, but a pure reflex.

It's delirium, essentially.

It is a technological delirium, but not just the delirium of the "Formula One" driver in his race car. It is the delirium of the politician, of all those who are trapped in this milieu of speed. I keep on saying it: speed is not only a problem of time, *it's a problem of milieu.* Speed is a milieu, and it even is *the* milieu. Everything that we have discussed concerning architecture shows that the milieu is not only spatio-temporal, it is dromospherical. It is a milieu that is applied to the body of the earth by means of the human body. Tomorrow, however, it could be applied to just about anything. The great revelation, the great revolution, therefore, is *the dromological revolution.* No one can deny it. Dromology is beyond history in the sense of time, in the sense of chronology. I am not talking Fukuyama here. It is not history, but the historical tempo that has changed. And this acceleration of the tempo has become an acceleration of reality, modifying our relation to the real to the point that the question of teleportation has been raised. We discussed this a little while ago —not the decomposition and recomposition of atoms and molecules, but a transfer of presence and action at a distance. We are coming back to interactivity.

Is artificial intelligence still intelligence?

No. It's a computation, as they say. And I don't have anything against it either. But why call it intelligence? Is it not to say that this intelligence is superior to human's?

Our last hero, Professor Warwick, the microchip man, wouldn't doubt that it is. Unlike Steve Mann, he seems totally thrilled at the thought that humans will be superseded by highly intelligent machines. Actually, Warwick suggested, if machines are more intelligent than us, why not enlist cybernetics to "buy a little more time for ourselves"? What about linking people's nervous system to a computer, by-passing the eyes and opening a whole new range of senses? Signals from the implant would be converted to digital, which opens the possibility of any kind of manipulation, including exchanging emotion signals, even pains signals, from one person to another... From there could evolve a cyborg community *via chip implants linked to superintelligent machines, "creating, in efffect, superhumans." Warwick had an early start. He was already dreaming of robots in the crib and couldn't wait until he became one. "What happens," he wondered, "when humans merge with machines? ... Those who have become cyborgs will be one step ahead of humans..*"[48]

Every time we question artificial intelligence, they object: "C'mon, a man can't calculate fast enough, so we invented this thingamabob that goes faster." But once you have said that, you haven't said anything. It isn't because it goes faster that it's better. We know that too well. So, artificial intelligence is a way of discrediting reflection in favor of calculation. You know to what extent I believe the material and the spiritual to be linked. I'm not a believer in metempsychosis, but I don't think one can separate the body from the mind. So I don't think one can improve the body without worrying about what is called the spirit. And the intervention of artificial intelligence, or to call it by its name, *the information bomb*, cannot be a gradual event. And this is unacceptable. Artificial intelligence is an aberration—it's not of the same nature. From this perspective, the cognitive sciences are an absurdity. The only cognitive scientist with whom I could talk was Francisco Varella because he was a phenomenologist. I am a phenomenologist, and I never stopped being one. I always said as much to Deleuze and the others. In my opinion, Husserl is worth ten times Heidegger. It is about time to wake up, moreover, since we are in the process of forgetting Husserl and phenomenology, when in fact we have never gone beyond it. That is what is so terrible. If we had gone beyond it, I would be the first to forget it. But we have not gone beyond it, we have left it to the machine. Precisely, through artificial intelligence, through cognitivism, etc. And it's an illusion. It is part of the deskilling that we talked about a little while ago.

What has been assumed is that the speed of the machine is in the service of humanity.

Yes, of course. After two centuries, what service has it done us?

Total Accident

The genetic manipulation of humans is the accident of science.

In some way, the accident of science is an accident that has not yet taken place, even if we can say that the labs—I mean the labs, not extermination, not the gas chambers—the labs at Auschwitz-Birkenau were the prefiguration of this accident. Auschwitz was not only a crime against humanity; it is the beginning of the accident of science. Now I am working exclusively on this notion of accident.

You said earlier that the militarization of knowledge led to the politics of the very worst. Is the accident of science going to be the accident of politics as well? Could it even be said that the accident is going to be the pursuit of politics by other means?

It is no longer a traditional war with armies that is going to continue politics in the way Clausewitz described it. It is the accident, but the Total Accident. We are standing before a kind of putsch. It is the military-scientific putsch, not the putsch of a few generals. If the accident is the continuation of politics by other means, one realizes to what extent this is the reversal of the geo-political and philosophical thought of both Machiaveli and Clausewitz. So, all by itself, this is a massive event in thought. One can spend a lifetime on this. What I am saying, and I think I am the first to say it, is that *the accident is the new form of warfare*. This is enough to continue the Greco-Latin and the Judeo-Christian model. But here we are coming back to the word "apocalypse." What is the Bible? It is a book of war. It never stops in the Old Testament. The massacres never stop. Furthermore, this fact has shocked many people, including l'Abbé Pierre and Simone Weil: Joshua has the sun stop its course so as to continue fighting, they turn the shields to blind their attackers—well, it's nothing but war. How is God called in the Old Testament? The God of Armies. I remind you that this same God is my own. It is not only the God of the Jews: it is theirs and mine. It is the same one. There is no other. So what does all this mean? It means that the Bible is the book of the Apocalypse. It means that the Apocalypse is happening all the time, everyday, since Genesis. It never stops. *Man is the end of the world*. That is what it means. Then in the end you have the New Testament, you have Christ, and then you have the Apocalypse. *Alles fertig*. History is following this same course, there is no doubt about it. Except that science plays a big part in it.

Simone Weil was revolted by the thought that the God of the Old Testament as well as the Hebrews would have condoned the massacre of the Canaanites by Joshua. And Emmanuel Levinas replied that God didn't justify such a cruelty. On the contrary, He was exposing His people to the absolute horror of blood.

"War is the mother of all things."

War may be the mother of all things, but it is no longer the Mother of all Wars. The nature of war has completely changed. And this mutation came out of the Second World War the way speed came out of the First World War.

Exactly.

War is not going to follow anymore the model of Kosovo and its massacres.

No, Kosovo was a little operation, just a battlefield. War is the accident. Look how we ended the Second World War: with an accident. We were told that these were bombs. I wish they were. In reality these were not bombs. *They exterminated science.* Hiroshima and Nagasaki didn't destroy two cities: it was the beginning of the extermination of science. And with the information bomb and the genetic bomb, they will finish the job.

The Very Worst

Simone Weil kept reflecting simultaneously on politics and science, going all the way back to Greek geometry.

You are right to take an interest in these women who are liberating rather than liberated. Because they have things to tell us. They had some idea of the accident of science, the accident of politics, the accident of knowledge—a much more precise idea than others. If we separate science from philosophy and religion, it is because of specialization. And it is by specializing that we began to destroy science. This is the reason we were forced to invent automatons.

So, the apotheosis of science is the apocalypse of science.

The best of things is the worst of things. This is always the case. Good and evil cannot be separated. That is why Aesop's phrase is still excellent. When people ask me what I think of computer science and the cyber bomb, cybernetics, cyberspace. I answer with the same phrase that Aesop did: What is the best of things? Information technology. What is the worst of things? Information technology. Today we are faced with a kind of slack-jawed optimism with respect to new technologies, which is for me perhaps the latest conformism. Good and evil tend to be replaced by optimism. Optimism is good, and pessimism is evil. It's an academic form of ethics. Academic and media-friendly. And a thinker cannot be an optimist, or he isn't thinking. That's why I said that genetics is the best and the worst. Obviously, the possibilities of control over the "book of life," of decoding the human genome, can promote the treatment for diseases. But we know very well that those techniques are quickly used to treat people in perfect health. [*laughs*]. We know that. You can see it happening with Viagra. Viagra is for the impotent. Do you really think that those who are taking it are impotent? Of course not! It's a stimulant. And it is the same thing every time we invent a technology. Its aspects are always presented in a positive light, an optimist light, but they mask the negative dimensions. And they can't be masked. We're living in a double-bind. Technology is a double-bind. There is no

progress without progress of the catastrophe. At the beginning
we invent a new technology, and we end up rendering natural
fertility sterile to make money. There you have it.

*Do you think that science could manage to police itself in some way?
Would it be even possible to try and reinforce its more positive aspect?
Could there be something like a positive "eugenics" of science?*

Now, you don't have to ask me that. What is censorship today? It's
advertising. When they tell me: "What you are saying is horrible,"
I say: "Do you know how many billions of dollars advertising
commits to its campaigns each year? Six hundred billions." The
power of censorship goes by the name of advertising, or "communication." The power of silence is much more extraordinary
today than it ever was. What is my critique compared to the pro-
motion of the New Age and the trans-human? The whole positive
side of this research has been developed in books, television
shows, cults, techno-cults, techno-parades, etc. So, the only way
to be free is to reject optimism. Like Aesop. You are familiar with
Hildegard de Bingen's sentence—I said it at the death of Heiner
Müller, and I will repeat it here. Hildegard de Bingen was the
extraordinary woman, poet and musician, born nine hundred
years ago today, who used to be a teacher to the king of her day
in her convent on the banks of the Rhine—a kind of Christian
Lorelei. Her great phrase is. *Homo est closula mirabilium Dei.*
What does it mean? "Humanity is the conclusion of God's won-
ders." Period. The key word is conclusion, *closula.* This woman—
and it is no accident that this is a woman—says that humans are
the end of the world. Not the heart of the world, not the center
of the world—she is not being anthropocentric, nor is she being
geocentric; these are views that have often been wrongly attached

to Christianity, to Judeo-Christianism. Hildegard de Bingen is saying just the opposite. She is saying that humans are the end of creation. But "end" is understood in the sense of "closula," a harsh word. I spoke to a Latinist about it. *Closula* is the ultimate aspect of humanity, not only in terms of catastrophe, but also power.

Human is the End

What does this expression "humanity is the end of the world" actually mean?

Let's make sure we understand one another here. The end does not mean the end of the world. It means the end of *a* world. In other words, the world proper that has made history is in the process of coming to a close. And the conclusion of the world proper, it is *homo est closula*. The revelation of the body also provoked the end. But humans provoked this conclusion through techno-scientific progress, the progression of the techno-sciences. The conclusion is in us and before us. We are living the conclusion rather than the end. There is no going beyond humanity. Humans are the conclusion, that is, they *close* the world. They are the ones who puts an end to the world. They conclude it. Humanity is the end. In other words, they are at once the perfection, the ones who bring an end, who take responsibility: whence the incarnation of Christ. At the same time, however, humanity is what ends it. So, you see, when you say humans are the end of the world, you can think of it as something negative, and at the same time you can think of it as something positive. Humans are not central in the history of the universe. They are terminal. It's all over. It is all over with humanity. This is acquired knowledge in Judeo-Christianism and early philosophy. Whence the importance of the Greeks. There is no genetic progress of being. One cannot improve humans by genetic means. There is no trans-human. There is only the infra-human. This is the Christian talking. Hence all this research, in my opinion, can only lead to a catastrophe of science itself, to the death of science, or if you prefer, to the Total Accident of science. So, for me, there is no going beyond humanity. There are no super-humans. And those who say, "But we can discover a better human," well, they have chosen their camp. I am not saying this in a moral way: there is no possibility of improving humanity by the techniques. I am an absolute anti-eugenicist.

So the perfect human in fact is an inferior human.

We saw it with the Nazis: in certain religions, or certain visions of religion, or certain visions of ideology, the super-human is the perfect human. And we have seen the catastrophe that this vision brought, in the exterminations, whether it is the extermination of the Jews or—well, it is pointless to go over it again. Humanity is the end of the world, and it is also is an end in the ethical sense of the word. This is where Nazism comes back, but this time on a scale that is...

...planetary?

On a scale that we cannot even imagine.

Knowing the Facts

It seems that theory no longer even needs to project itself forward that much to apprehend phenomena: it is enough to bring together what already exists. As William Burroughs said, paranoia is knowing the facts. Theory is knowing the facts.

Theory is construction. Right now I am trying to understand the nature of the Total Accident—what I call the total or global accident. The old techniques in the transportation revolution provoked accidents that were specific, local. Invent the luxury liner, and you invent the "Titanic." Invent electricity, and you invent Chernobyl. These are local accidents. And I am deliberately saying that Chernobyl is a local accident. Even if the melt-down contaminates Europe, it is still a local accident. On the other hand, by virtue of cybernetic technologies, the accident is total. It simultaneously concerns the entire world at the same instant. The colossal dimension of the accident surpasses us, and that's why I am so passionate about it.

Once we discussed the accident in terms of the stock-market crash.

Yes, that is an image of instantaneity. What crumbled in the crash is obviously a system of values—it is science itself. Science is in danger of dying. It is going to be next

How could it die?

First I will say: *by an excess of speed.* When we denounce the computer and artificial intelligence, what is it that we are denouncing? We are not against machines and robots, that's just fairy tales. Rather, the excess of speed can be a denial of science. If one considers that speed is a power, this power can supplant all the others, including the power of scientific knowledge. This excess of speed goes through the ideology of artificial intelligence and robotics, but it goes farther than that. Much farther. And this, too, is part of the Total Accident. This is a logic which is difficult to analyze, because the accident of science that we were just discussing is linked to this total accident.

And the total accident is the other name for the absolute interactivity that regulates information, free trade and the global market.

It is linked to the cybernetic dimension of information, so it is quite complex. The work remains to be done on it. But I believe that there is nothing else to do now than to scope out its negative dimension. Contrary to the many who tell me that critique is no longer possible, I say: the opposite is true; there is no longer anything possible, *except* critique. Only critique is possible now, precisely because we no longer have the power to stem these tendencies. Why not? Because we can no longer fall back on a philosophical power or on a religious power in the broad sense of wisdom.

Runaway Train

There are as well powerful interests at stake: corporations, multinationals... But is there something in science itself that would actually prevent us from curbing all this?

In my opinion, it's speed. The rapidity of a phenomenon liquidates you. When a phenomenon reaches an absolute speed, it sets a "runaway" in motion. This is true in every field—if you walk by a billboard slowly, you can read it; if you go by really fast, you see nothing. But this is no longer happening at a personal level. This stunning effect of speed is being felt through and in power itself. The power of speed has become more potent than the power of wealth. The two are linked, of course. Time is money, and speed is power. Today, the power of absolute speed, of live transmission, of cybernetic information technology is such that traditional power, which used to rely on force, on armies, on police, etc., and even on wealth, can no longer hold it back. *The "runaway" is under way.* This is a state of emergency.

This is simultaneously true of every field. Genetics will make trees grow more quickly, abolish the seasons, anticipate evolution...

It's theater. It's the *deus-ex-machina*, a theater machine, which is being carried out on a global scale. The machine used to be nothing more than speed. Today it is being applied to the real, to political reality, to sociological reality, and to the military reality, whence it came. Because don't forget that all of this came out of the scientific and military industrial complex. I will never forget what Eisenhower said, his last speech in 1961, when he was leaving the White House. He said: "Beware of the military-industrial complex. It can destroy all of our democratic values." Well, it's started. It's done. It is in the process of destroying everything.

We don't even need the competition between the East and West blocs anymore to destroy everything, or rather multiply exponentially our power of destruction.

No, it works all by itself. From this perspective, the Gulf War—you read my book—illustrated the search for a second deterrence. We cannot understand the test, the weapons maneuvers which took place in the Balkans, without the search for some other deterrence, which in effect would be based on the accident. The accident is going to become the pursuit of politics by other means. It is no longer a traditional war with armies that is going to continue politics in the way Clausewitz described it. It is the accident, *but the Total Accident*. The big mystery is the nature of this accident. And it goes hand in hand with the new deterrence. We are standing before a kind of putsch, but it is a military-scientific putsch, not the putsch of a few generals.

Now that the USSR has crumbled down, the search for an adversary —the so-called "rogue states," the specter of international terrorism —is this not pure theater. Obviously theater can be real too, all the better really if you want to keep occupying the stage.

Yes. In deterrence, the adversary is everybody else. When I spoke of first deterrence, with respect to the second which the Americans have been looking for, I was speaking of this honeymoon period when the United States was the only one to have the bomb, I mean that unprecedented moment in which one power had the possibility to control the entire world. It didn't last very long because, there were the Rosenbergs, and then bye-bye. So, I feel like saying that it is this search which is now in the works, any attempt to find once again new forms of deterrence. In other words, *block everything, control everything*. You could say that it is totally terroristic.

Imperial Illusion

Hence the decision by the American Senate, in 1999 not to sign the treaty against nuclear proliferation.

We can't understand its refusal otherwise.

At the moment, it seems to me that the American Empire is trying to maintain its dominance through a two-fold strategy: on the one hand, imposing globalization and free trade; on the other, perfecting its war technology. One strategy is to open up borders world-wide, the other to impose U.S. supremacy over the rest of the world. Clinton's carrot on one side and Bush Jr.'s stick on the other. The American wager is to use these two movements of deterritorialization like pliers, monitoring the turbulence that laissez faire *is creating throughout the world—local strife, fundamentalist threats, abysmal poverty, etc.—from the height of its electronic might.*

It is totally aberrant. It's totally utopian. As I said, you cannot compose with a decomposing society. Trying to keep decomposition at a distance is a misunderstanding of how chaos works. No one can remain immune from chaos, globalization being chaos extended to the totality of the world, including America, including each of us. Each one of us as a person, as a body, is subjected to the threat of chaos, or to real chaos. America like the others. America too is a decomposing country.

It has been founded on chaos from the very beginning. That's what America is.

Yes, yes. But what I really want to say is: we can save ourselves when the rest of the world is composed. But when we are in a decomposing world, when everything decomposes because of the acceleration of exchange, the deconstruction of instances and of institutions, then there is no future. Therefore I believe that it is an imperial illusion. It still is a geographical illusion, a naval illusion. America is a colony, actually the only colony that has never been colonized. Hence the role of the Navy in the United States, of aircraft carriers, etc. What is a colony? It means controlling a country by coasting around one's land. It is gunboat politics. And they forgot temporal compression, the fact that there is no more coasting, or that the last coasting now is aero-orbital. But this aero-orbital coasting can't solve the problem of social decomposition in the cities, of decomposition of the social fabric into anomy. Because we are not confronted with a Balkanic situation, we are in front of an *anomic* situation. The big threat, I realized it in 1968, is not anarchy, or Balkanization, but Sicilianization, that is, anomy. Everything is breaking down, organization, laws, communal values... Leonardo Sciascia used to say that that the world is threatened by Sicilianization, not Balkanization. And I would go even further and say that what threatens the decomposing world of globalization is anomy, and by this I mean the loss of references, the loss of all distinctions.

This goes together with the disqualification of a good portion of humanity under the pressure of the new technologies.

Decomposition is everywhere, everywhere. What is decomposing is the geographical space, the psychophysical and psychophysio-physical space of being. It affects at once the big territorial body, the small animal body and the social body. The social body is decomposing. You can tell by the end of the states, and maybe the end of the possibility of having a world-state, that is, a final state, a total state.

The American utopia.

Yes, the American utopia. And the last body, the animal body, not to say the human body itself, is subjected to two pressures. The pressure of the body proper, of the territorial body reduced to nothing, and the pressure of the decomposing social body, where structures of procreation, of production, and of course of resistance in any area, are themselves unsettled. And this, in the first stage, brings about the Mafia. This is happening now in Colombia, in Sierra Leone: anything goes.

Everything is interconnected.

In times to come, everything will be interactive. The general tendency, everything.

The American Empire can only assert its superiority by creating larval countries, monsters or chimeras on the political scale, and not just at the genetic level; by keeping conflicts simmering, so that they don't escalate beyond repair. In other words, managing mayhem.

And if I give you my feeling: America is done for. When I say America is done for, I mean that the world is done for. Globalization is a phenomenon that surpasses Americanization. Many of our old French Marxists. are still preoccupied with anti-Americanism or anti-first worldism. I believe that we are past all that. Globalization, this is the end of America.

When America becomes the world, the world is finished.

The world is finished and therefore America is finished. But all of this goes way beyond the White House. We are faced with a phenomenon that is a runaway train. And this applies as well to transgenic plants, and transgenic beings.

And this does not concern the United States alone.

No.It involves the whole world. Everybody.

So, in a certain way, that's where we're headed to.

We're on our way.

It's all over, we're on our way. The runaway is on the way.

Paris/New York, November 1999-May 2001

EPILOGUE: CREPUSCULAR DAWN

Unabomber □ Mass Killer □ The Accident-Weapon □ Anthropological Horizons □ Chernobyl and the World Trade Center □ The Great Attack

Did you like the Unabomber Manifesto?

Theodore Kazinski is an interesting character. Honestly, when I finished reading it, I thought: I would have liked to meet this guy, I would have had a few things to tell him.

Actually he says many things you could have said yourself.

I can't say that I am simply opposed to it... Terrorism forget it, I'm against that. But the part where he analyzes the crisis of industrial society as catastrophic, I couldn't agree more. I was surprised by the accuracy of his analysis. It recalls Jacques Ellul and Jonas—the principle of responsibility—and all the critics of contemporary civilization, including some aspects of Hannah Arendt.

I agree entirely. The problem is that he relies on the internal contradictions of capitalist society, as if capitalist society did not thrive off its contradictions. It's a dialectical exorcism. It doesn't lead to anything specific either, so he comes up with the revolution.

That's when, for me, it's over...

He got short of ideas.

He described very well the stalemate situation, the foreclosure of industry, the contraction of the world, so that if things keep going the way they are, it's all going to explode. But you don't need a revolution for that.

He must not have believed it would all explode either, otherwise why urge us to destroy the industrial system now, before it has entirely set in? The explosions he set off himself with his letter-bombs were a poor substitute for that, and it was not revolution, merely assassination. The programmatic aspect of his Manifesto *anyway, on the whole, is pretty lame.*

The second part, where he speaks in his own name, what a disaster! This subtle, intelligent man, who puts his finger on a number of things, is an idiot when it comes to proposing anything. You feel like grabbing him and saying: "Cut it out, will you!" How can he say such extraordinary things when it comes to criticism, and then on the other hand, nothing.

Maybe you could rewrite the second part yourself...

Oh no, I wouldn't know where to begin.

But you would know where it ends.

No. For me nothing is preordained. In this sense, I still have hope. The three bombs have the power to snuff out their source, but this power is potential. Within the information bomb, the atomic bomb and the genetic bomb, it is possible to get inside the system and to deal with it in a different way. To get inside the software. In my opinion, that's what our job is: to wrestle with the genetic bomb as human beings—not as gods. To wrestle with the information bomb so as to produce something other than cybernetics. To wrestle with the atom bomb so as to avoid blowing everything to kingdom come. So, I don't believe that the world is finished, either. I am not a nihilist. I am simply saying that we have to fight like Jacob. Each person must wrestle with the angel. It is an awesome fight, a fight much more important than the Unabomber's fight. Precisely, it is what the Unabomber did not do. I am waiting for a Unabomber named Jacob.

Jacob wrestled with the angel, but he didn't kill him with letter-bombs.

Mass Killer

Precisely. That's why I see the Mass Killer in the Unabomber—the Mass Killer as the great criminal, even if there is an ideology behind him. There is Theodore Kazinski's phrase after his arrest: "For people to remember, there have to be a great many victims."

Hitler started that, and he was pretty successful. Now he is even becoming a CBS Entertainment blockbuster. Young Hitler, the lonely adolescent...

You find the same exact sentence in Durn, the man who massacred the entire city council in Nanterre. He just went back to
Town Hall, killed them all and then killed himself by jumping
out the window. Behind this you have an effect of exemplarity,
which Kazinski articulated: "I want them to remember me..."
The exemplarity of crime which will lead to hyper-terrorism, the
criminality against humanity. Right now we're dealing with two
suicide-jetliners; tomorrow it will be a radiological bomb—the
so-called "dirty" bomb—that will make New York, Paris, or
London uninhabitable. This year, in Paris, they arrested people
who were negotiating the sale of uranium in their own home. So,
it's unavoidable. It won't be the atomic bomb, Hiroshima,
boom—no, it will be the radiological bomb. What interests me
about the Mass Killer is this mass effect. For us to remember,
there have to be mass victims—and mass media.

The Mass Killer is a creature of the mass media, and we're all victims.
In any case this is classical terrorist logic applied to mass assassina-
tion. The Red Army Fraction and the Red Brigades were more
selective in their killings, but they were going for the media as well.
They hadn't realized that the media already were the masses, or
maybe they already realized it all too well.

What we have here is a phenomenon of crime modeling, and the
World Trade Center is just one more confirmation of it.
Mohamed Atta and his colleagues crashed into the WTC; the kid
from Bishop took off from Tampa and crashed into the Bank of
America, after flying over the base where the command-control
for the war on Afghanistan was located. He was fifteen, he
washed planes. He barely knew how to pilot a plane, and he
played at make-believe: "I'm Bin Laden." Then there's the Italian

who rammed his plane into a sky-scraper in Milan. They said it was an accident... They think we're stupid. It's not an Islamic attack, it's a modeling effect. Once you have two, you start to have more. This is the quantitative logic of the media. The media works only *en masse*, by means of a mass effect. In the Unabomber you have a forerunner of this world terrorism, and that is what makes it interesting. He should be interviewed, too. Tell him: "Listen, pal, we don't give a damn about your story now that you're in prison. But what do you think about the World Trade Center?" Plus he looks conceited. Did you see him? An extraordinary presence. Admit it, he's interesting.

Bin Laden looked very interesting too. Kazinski suggested that the task that confronts "those who hate servitude" is to heighten social stresses by a host of therapeutic shocks. September 11 was quite a therapy.

In a sense, the new terrorists are bringing all this to fruition. And they're only getting started. The World Trade Center is the dawn of a new war.

The Accident-Weapon

A war which, obviously, will no longer speak its name.

Exactly. But the great danger is the confusion of the attack with the accident. As soon as the terrorist becomes anonymous, as soon as he refuses to declare war and refuses to declare himself, and these acts go unclaimed, or the terrorist dies and he simply can't tell his story, the attack and the accident in some way become indistinguishable. It's a revolution in the art of war

VIRILIO / LOTRINGER

which goes back, I would say, to the invention of gun powder. It changes everything. *You can't win a war if you can't recognize the enemy.* This is an incredible event. The attack in Toulouse remains unclaimed to this day. Incertitude is even more dangerous, because they closed the factory. Now there are conflicts in the city...

Can the accident be a substitute for terrorism in the end?

In this case, yes. The accident is the new form of warfare. I had already said so concerning the graphite bombs over Belgrade. The new bombs are not weapons... What are weapons? They are instruments that create accidents, they are machines that provoke accidents. They are not accident machines. They are productive, destructive machines. When the Americans invent the graphite bomb to plunge an entire country into darkness, a black-out, they are in some way rehearsing the Total Accident; they're no longer playing at destruction. The same goes for the neutron bomb. With the neutron bomb, it's not about destruction. Everything just has to be uninhabitable. That way there's no more problem. So, in this case, it's the same logic. They're using the accident instead of using explosives. It can be an electrical black-out, it can be a cybernetic bomb, *but a real one*, that will cause a cybernetic meltdown. A cybernetic bomb could be a massive energy black-out: imagine if you could cut the electricity of the entire world all at the same time, you see it in science fiction. It's an incredible catastrophe by domino-effect. This is the logic we are in: with graphite bombs, the Americans are looking for an accident-weapon; and on the other side, the terrorists have just used the same technique.

Chernobyl and the World Trade Center

But in miniature.

Still, there were more deaths than in Pearl Harbor. Think about it. At Pearl Harbor there was an armada, air-craft carriers, etc., the Japanese killed two thousand and six hundred people. In this case, with Bin Laden, we have three thousand dead with two planes crashing into two towers. And it was a miracle that the two buildings stood as long as they did. Under normal circumstances, the impact and the fire should have taken down the tower in fifteen minutes. I did an analysis of it on the "France-Culture" radio with a few French engineers. First the impact could have knocked them over, since there was no cement core. In France, for this very reason, you are obligated to build with a core. It's like a tree trunk: when there is no core, an impact of that force can knock them down. Had the towers been knocked down, there would have been forty thousand dead in one blow. About twenty thousand per tower. And then those below, can you imagine? So let's say fifty thousand dead, maybe sixty thousand. You're getting close to Hiroshima: seventy thousand dead on impact. And they didn't even talk about the casualties from radiation contamination. seventy thousand dead from the explosion of the bomb in Hiroshima, Nagasaki is slightly less. The Twin Towers withstood the impact, and the fire, for an hour—which is amazing for a metal structure. Amazing. You know how it happens. Metal structures catch fire, not in the sense that they burn, but the walls warp, and the ceilings fall. And one three thousand square foot ceiling that falls brings down a second, and they bring down the others, and it goes clack, clack, clack... that's what we saw. So, one hour saved thirty thousand people, at least. It was thanks to the firemen, and to providence—I say providence, because technically the towers shouldn't have lasted an hour. Fire-protection, shock-protection. A kerosene fire was overlooked by the engineers. They foresaw furniture fires, electrical fires, power surges: *The Towering Inferno* doesn't get you very far...

What about the materials...

The thousands of windows that had just shattered, the other thousand windows with kerosene burning, it all shoots up the temperature. The New York fire fighters are real heroes and deserve a wall like the soldiers of Vietnam, I hope they'll give them one. This is the same heroism as those Soviets who poured cement over the Chernobyl reactor to bury it. It cost them their lives. I was with Svetlana Alexinievich yesterday, and she told me that. About a thousand men from the army were sacrificed, fire fighters, they came to pour cement for hours on end. If they hadn't done it, the critical mass would have exploded. And the critical mass at Chernobyl would be eighty times Hiroshima. Half of Europe would be uninhabitable. About a thousand of these liquidators died—they call them "liquidators," that's the term they use.

Didn't they have protection?

Yes. But they went to the heart of the thing. They would have had to wear lead, diving-suits, but they were running too fast to do that. I spoke with Svetlana for two hours yesterday—you know her book, *La Supplication*. She has given us an unprecedented account of it. They performed it as a play in Avignon, too. She met the Soviet fire fighters, and she recorded their eye-witness accounts before they died. Some helicopter pilots burned because they were so oxidized by the radiation. These guys are real heroes too, we should remember them together. Svetlana said that for her Chernobyl was the greatest historical accident of the twentieth century, and now the only thing comparable is the World Trade Center. That's when I realized we were facing new phenomena. The ecologists are not up to the job. In fact, we are headed towards an eschatological party. A Party of the End. Not the end of the world, but finitude, enclosure.

The end by technology...

By technology and its damage.

We've come full circle to the Unabomber.

Anthropological Horizons

This is not pessimism, but political realism. An anthropological horizon of expectations exists. It used to be Messianism, the great fear of the Middle Ages. It also was Millenarism, which is something else entirely. But if we take the modern period, there are three horizons. In the 18th century, the horizon of expectations is starting with the *Great Revolution*. First the English revolution, then 1789, all the way to the October Revolution on up to the implosion of the USSR, which marks the end of the revolutionary horizon of expectations. Revolution won't be back. It is foreclosed, globalization has outflanked it. The original horizon of expectations has spawned many revolutions—the industrial revolution, the bourgeois revolution, the October revolution, etc. This is progress. The second horizon of expectations to come out of it was the *Great War* of 1914. It is still is political, but it goes beyond Clausewitz. We got three Great Wars: WWI, with the assassination in Sarajevo; WWII, with Auschwitz, Hiroshima; and the undeclared WWIII: the Cold War, the race to death, deterrence, the equilibrium of terror, Mutual Assured Destruction, (MAD). With the Third Great War, the second horizon of expectations came to an end. The third is the *Great Accident*, whose first party is the ecological party. Except the party doesn't really translate the horizon of expectations very well. It's too preoccupied with pollution, flowers, birds, acid rain. The accident is much more than that: it's about the accident of knowledge, the Total Accident, the Great Accident. It's here, it's on the way. Revolution, War, Accident, all these things are interconnected. It's telescopic, like a fishing pole.

So, after the Accident there will be no others?

For the moment. This is the dawn of the third horizon. I think the ecological party prefigures an eschatological party, the Party of the End. And in some way, world terrorism is connected to it. That explains its suicidal character. And let me just say that the suicidal aspect is not at all Arab, or Muslim, or French…

It's Japanese. Michael Prazan documented it in his recent book, Les Fanatiques, *on the Japanese Red Army. It's a horror story. They apparently picked up where WWII kamikaze pilots left it.*[49]

Yes. The *Zengaturen* [Radical Student Committee] and the Japanese Red Army [*Nihon Sekigun*] infiltrated the Palestinian FPLP. One of the leaders of the Japanese terrorist movement is

Fusako Shigenobu, who was arrested in 2000 and is imprisoned right now in Japan. She was a passionaria known as the "Red Queen." She came to the Middle East in 1969 after hijacking a plane from the Japan Airlines and she is the one who contaminated the Palestinian terrorists. Who *inseminated* them—that is the word for it—with the suicidal terrorist attack. It's an absolute scandal. The suicidal terrorist attack has nothing to do with Islam or with Christianity. When people speak of the "martyrs," it's their way of Islamicizing the Japanese suicide attack. And do you know when this woman was born?

It must have been at the time of Hiroshima...

On September 20, 1945, one month after Hiroshima. You have to admit...

I recently watched an early film directed by Shoheo Imamura on Hiroshima, Black Rain. *I saw it just after the attack of 9-11 to be precise. In New York, there were almost three thousand victims, but no one thought of bringing up Hiroshima at the time. So now we're no longer talking about hijackings...*

The Great Attack

No. The whole scale has changed. We have set foot in the *Great Attack,* at least that's what they're aiming at... Today anything is possible. As soon as you get beyond hijackings and car bombs, things like that, you entertain the possibility of nuclear, bacteriological, or chemical terrorism. The door is wide open. September 11 opened Pandora's Box. In this new situation, New York is what Sarajevo was. Sarajevo triggered the First

World War. New York is the attack in the first war of globalization. An internecine war, a civil war that has nothing to do with
the Clausewitzian forms of war...

Civil war has become world war...

...and it no longer has anything to do with previous forms of
war, the flags, declarations of war, uniforms, or news bulletins
of victory. In this sense, the American army, the U.S. Armed
Forces, the U.S. Air Force, ah, they're no use. The plane that
crashed into the Pentagon is an example. In a sense, America is
already behind by one war.

Paris, May 2002

NOTES

1. Georges Bataille, "Reflexions sur le bourreau et la victime" [Reflections on the Torturer and the Victim], in *Oeuvres Complètes* XI. Paris: Gallimard, 1988, p. 264.

2. Paul Virilio, *Bunker Archeology*: Texts and Photos, trans. George Collins (New York: Princeton Architectural Press, 1994).

3. Paul Virilio, *The Politics of the Very Worst*. Trans. Michael Cavaliere. New York: Semiotext(e) Foreign Agents Series, 1999. [La Politique du pire. Paris: Editions Textuels, 1996].

4. See Paul Virilio/Sylvère Lotringer, *Pure War*, trans. Mark Polizotti, postscript trans. Brian O'Keefe/ New York: Semiotext(e) Foreign Agents, 1983; reprint 1997.

5. Paul Virilio/Claude Parent, *Architecture Principe*: 1966 and 1996, trans. George Collins (Besançon: Les Editions de l'Imprimeur, 1997).

6. "Tallboys" are bombs specially conceived to bust bunkers.

7. André Bloc was the founding father of *L'Architecture d'Aujourd'hui* and collaborated with Parent in *Groupe Espace*, which tried to merge architecture and art. [E.N.]

8. Virilio doesn't mention that Le Corbusier actually loved New York skyscrapers and wished they were higher. [E.N.]

9. Circadian rhythms are biological rhythms which remain constant during a period of 24 hours independently of the actual duration of day or night.

10. Michel Siffre, *Beyond Time*. New York: McGraw-Hill, 1964.

11. Paul Virilio, *Speed and Politics*. Trans. Mark Polizzotti. New York: Semiotext(e) Foreign Agents, 1986. [*Vitesse et Politique*. Paris:Galilée, 1977]

12. Paul Virilio, *L' Insécurité du territoire*. Paris: Stock, 1976; Paris: Galilée, 1993.

13. Paul Virilio, *Lost Dimension*. Trans. Daniel Moshenberg. New York: Semiotext(e) Foreign Agents, 1991. [*L'Espace critique*. Paris:Christian Bourgois, 1984].

14. Henri Lefèbvre, *La Revolution urbaine*. Paris: Gallimard, 1970.

15. Henri Lefèbvre, *Critique of Everyday Life*. London: Verso, 1991.

16. Henri Lefèbvre, *Eléments de Rythmanalyse*. Paris: Syllepse-Périscope, 1992.

17. "Dromology," logic of the race. From Greek, *dromos*, race, speed.

18. Paul Virilio/Sylvère Lotringer, *Pure War. op. cit.*

19. Paul Virilio, *Open Sky*. New York/London: Verso, 1997. [*La Vitesse de liberation*. Paris: Galilée, 1995].

20. After they broke of, Parent drew the ground as a female figure. [E.N.]

21. Paul Virilio, "Métempsychose du passager," *Traverses* #8, May 1977 (Centre Beaubourg): "Man is the passenger of woman, not only at birth, but also in sexual relations... The female is the means the male has found to reproduce himself, in other words, to come into the world. In this respect, woman is the species' first means of transport, its very first vehicle..."

22. Paul Virilio, *Polar Inertia*. London: Sage Publications, 2000. [*L'Inertie polaire*. Paris: Bourgois, 1990].

23. François Quesnay, a doctor and economist (1694-1774), was a main figure of the "physiocrats" group with Diderot, Turgot, Mirabeau and Dupont de Nemours, who opposed mercantilism and advocated abiding by natural laws and saw real wealth in natural products, not in money. Quesnay compared the circulation of goods and services to the circulation of blood in the human body.

24. William Forsythe is the artistic director of the Frankfurt Ballet. A disciple of Rudolf von Laban and of architect Daniel Libeskind, he experiments with elements breaking down the unity of movement.

25. Paul Virilio, *Popular Defense and Ecological Struggles*, Trans. Mark Polizzotti. New York: Semiotext(e) Foreign Agents, 1990. [*Défense populaire et luttes écologiques*. Paris:Galilée, 1978].

26. Paul Virilio/ Jacqueline Salmon, *Chambres précaires*. Heidelberg: Kehrer Verlag, 2000.

27. "Foreclosure," Lacan's translation for Freud's concept of *Verwerfung*: rejection, refusal, exclusion, a mechanism characteristic of paranoia. Virilio suggests, more phenomenologically, the spatial feeling of being locked-in, closed off, separated, surrounded.

28. Paul Virilio/Sylvère Lotringer, *Pure War. op. cit.*, ch. 7.

29. See: Bruce Schechter, "Real Life Cyborg Challenges Reality With Technology," *The New York Times*, September 25, 2001; Lisa Guernsey, "At Airport gate, a Cyborg Unplugged," ibid, March 14, 2002.

30. Francis Galton, *Hereditary Genius*. London: Macmillan and Co, 1925. Preface to the edition of 1892.

31. Robert Antelme, *The Human Race*. Marlboro, Vt: The Marlboro Press, 1992, p. 219.

32. Julia Kristeva, *Powers of Horror: An Essay on Abjection*. New York: Columbia University Press, 1982.

33. Giorgio Agamben. *Homo Sacer*. Paris: Editions du Seuil, 1997.

34. Ernst Klee, *La Medecine nazie et ses victimes*. Aix-en-Provence: Actes Sud, 1999.

35. Stefan Kuehl, *The Nazi Connection: Eugenics, American racism and German National Socialism*. New York: Oxford University press, 1994, p. 60.

36. Paul Virilio, *Un Paysage d'événements*. Paris:: Galilée,1996.

37. Fabulous monster, half-bull, half human, fed with human flesh.

38. Jean-François Lyotard, *The Unhuman*. Palo Alto: Stanford University Press, 1992.

39. An allusion to General Aussaresses, who recently bragged of having systematically tortured prisoners in Algeria, knowing that he was protected by the status of limitations. In 2001, he finally was condemned for "advocating violence." See his memoir, *Pour la France: Services speciaux: 1942-1954*. Paris: Plon, 2001.

40. Francis Fukuyama, *Our Post-Human Future*. New York: Farrar, Straus and Giroux, 2002.

41.Didier Pavy, "Les écorchés du docteur von Hagens." in *Nouvel Observateur,* October 2001.

42.*Visible Human Collection,* by Research Systems, Boulder, Colorado, 2000.

43. On "biological art," see the special issue of *Art Press*, February 2002, particularly Dominique Lestel's article, "The Artistic Manipulation of the Living."

44. Paul Virilio, *Procedure silence*. Paris: Editions Galilée, 2002. Procedure silence was the mechanism set up by the Allies during the war in Kosovo to approve the bombings. Silence meant acceptance.

45. *Auschwitz seen by the SS. Rudolf Hoess, Pery Broad, Johann Paul Kremer.* Oswiecim: The State Museum of Auschwitz-Birkenau, 1994

46. Gilles Deleuze/Félix Guattari, "Rhizome," in *On the Line.* New York: Semiotext(e) Foreign Agents series, 1983.

47. Paul Virilio, *Politics of the Very Worst.* New York: Semiotext(e) Foreign Agents, 2000.

48. Kevin Warwick, "Cyborg 1.05," in *Wired Magazine*, February 2000.

49. Michael Prazan, *Les Fanatiques. Histoire de l'Armee Rouge Japonaise.* Paris: Editions du Seuil, 2002.

SEMIOTEXT(E) • NATIVE AGENTS SERIES
Chris Kraus, *Editor*

Airless Spaces Shulamith Firestone
Aliens & Anorexia Chris Kraus
Hannibal Lecter, My Father Kathy Acker
How I Became One of the Invisible David Rattray
If You're a Girl Anne Rower
I Love Dick Chris Kraus
Indivisible Fanny Howe
Leash Jane DeLynn
The Madame Realism Complex Lynne Tillman
The New Fuck You: Adventures In Lesbian Reading Eileen
           Myles & Liz Kotz, eds
Not Me Eileen Myles
The Origin of the Species Barbara Barg
The Pain Journal Bob Flanagan
**The Passionate Mistakes and Intricate Corruption of One Girl
           in America** Michelle Tea
Reading Brooke Shields: The Garden of Failure Eldon Garnet
Walking Through Clear Water in a Pool Painted Black Cookie
           Mueller

SEMIOTEXT(E) • DOUBLE AGENTS SERIES
Sylvère Lotringer, *Editor*

Aesthetics of Disappearance Paul Virilio
Archeology of Violence Pierre Clastres
Burroughs Live (The Collected Interviews) Sylvère Lotringer, ed.
Desert Islands and Other Texts (1953-1974) Gilles Deleuze
Fatal Strategies Jean Baudrillard
Foucault Live: Collected Interviews of Michel Foucault Sylvère
Lotringer, ed.
Hatred of Capitalism: A Semiotext(e) Reader Chris Kraus &
Sylvère Lotringer, eds.
Lost Dimension Paul Virilio

SEMIOTEXT(E) • THE JOURNAL
Sylvère Lotringer, *Editor*

Imported: A Reading Seminar Rainer Ganahl, ed.
Polysexuality Francois Péraldi, ed.

Printed in the United States
by Baker & Taylor Publisher Services